THE ASHES

A FRONT ROW SEAT TO AN ICONIC ERA OF CRICKET IN THE '60s

MARK BROWNING

Published by:
Wilkinson Publishing Pty Ltd ACN 006 042 173
PO Box 24135
Melbourne, Vic 3001
Ph: 03 9654 5446
enquiries@wilkinsonpublishing.com.au
www.wilkinsonpublishing.com.au

Title: The Ashes: A Front Row Seat To An Iconic Era Of Cricket In The '60s
ISBN: 9781921804182

A catalogue record for this book is available from the National Library of Australia.

Cover design and internal design by Spike Creative
Printed and bound in Australia by Ligare Book Printers

CONTENTS

FOREWORD BY GREG CHAPPELL

When Mark Browning asked me to contribute a foreword to this book, I found myself transported back – not just to the pitches of the 1960s and early 70s, but to the backyards of Adelaide, where a boyhood dream was kindled under the almond trees and the stern yet loving gaze of my father, Martin. The Ashes, even then, was no mere cricket series. It was an idea – an inheritance. And like all things inherited, it demanded reverence, responsibility, and eventually, renewal.

Mark's book does something special. It retrieves an often-overlooked decade of Ashes cricket and views it not just through the lens of the scoreboard but through the social, cultural and personal upheavals that shaped – and nearly strangled – our most treasured rivalry. It asks us to reflect on a time when the Urn, for all its historic charm, teetered on irrelevance. Having lived through the tail end of that era, I can say this: we very nearly lost something priceless.

The 1960s were a strange liminal space for cricket. Australia was changing. England was changing. The world was changing. But the Ashes, for a time, did not. Cricket administrators seemed tethered to a version of the game – and of society – that was slipping away. Test matches dragged. Results were elusive. Public engagement waned. There were, believe it or not, serious conversations about whether the Ashes still mattered. For many of us, such an idea was sacrilege. Yet it was the reality.

I didn't begin that decade as a player. I began it as a kid. A dreamer. And usually, an Englishman – at least in our backyard Tests. Ian, my older brother and eternal tormentor, claimed Australia for himself, leaving me to assume the roles of Cowdrey, Dexter, and Evans. I lost often. But with every match – real or imagined – the Ashes embedded itself deeper in my soul.

By the end of the decade, I had graduated from those backyard battles to the national team. My debut came in the 1970/71 Ashes series, a period that now seems like a hinge moment for Australian cricket. Ian took over the captaincy from Bill Lawry, and with that came not just a new leadership style, but a new ethos. The old guard – grit and grind – was giving way to a more expressive, aggressive brand of cricket. It mirrored the changes we saw in society: long hair, louder music, and a growing demand for voice and individuality.

I was still learning the ropes, but the shift was unmistakable. The dressing room atmosphere changed almost overnight. Where once there had been a formality, now there was a sense of camaraderie and defiance. We were playing to win – but we were also playing to entertain. It wasn't reckless. It was real. And it was what the Ashes needed.

In those years, I was lucky to play alongside some extraordinary characters. Rod Marsh and Dennis Lillee, in particular, stood out. Rod was someone I first encountered at a schoolboy carnival – brash, intense, and unapologetically confident. I didn't warm to him immediately. But once we became teammates, I saw the depth of his commitment and the size of his heart. He was as tough as they come – keeping to Lillee and Thomson would have tested anyone – but he never flinched. He loved the team, and he loved the contest.

Dennis, of course, was a phenomenon. Fast, fierce, and unrelenting. But more than that, he was resilient. To come back from a serious back injury and reinvent himself as one of the great fast bowlers of all time speaks volumes. Together, Rod and Dennis were the heartbeat of a new era in Australian cricket – one built on belief, on honesty, and on the principle that cricket, like life, was meant to be played forward.

That's what made the 1972 Ashes series in England so special. It was, in many ways, the turning point. After a decade of doubt and drift, Ashes cricket roared back to relevance. The series was alive – every Test a battle, every session a test of skill and nerve. I remember it vividly because I was in the middle of it, both figuratively and literally. The century I scored at Lord's remains, to this day, the best innings I ever played. It was Bob Massie's Test, yes – but it was also the game where everything I had learned, every hard lesson from the backyard to Somerset, seemed to come together.

We didn't win the series outright, but we drew it 2-2, and we did so with style. That sixth day at The Oval – Rod Marsh and Paul Sheahan scampering through for the winning single – wasn't just a victory in the moment. It was a reclamation of the Ashes as an event. The Urn was back in the public imagination. Cricket had crossed the generational divide. Even Mick Jagger was there, pints in hand. And thanks to satellite television, fans back home in Australia could watch the drama unfold live – a far cry from the radio simulations I listened to as a boy.

It's tempting to see history in terms of heroes and results. But the truth is often more nuanced. The players of the 60s – Simpson, Booth, Cowdrey, Benaud – were fine cricketers and better men. They played in an era of transition and often took the brunt of public dissatisfaction. But they held the line. They protected the spirit of the game. Without them, there may have been no Ashes for us to revive.

I owe much of my cricketing education to those times. The County years with Somerset in the late 60s taught me humility and technique. Batting in English conditions was a different science altogether. The ball moved more. You had to earn every run. But it made me sharper, more adaptable. I don't think I'd have succeeded in 1972 without those formative years behind me.

And, of course, I had the privilege of growing up in a family that lived and breathed sport. My father, Martin, never played for South Australia – but he trained us like champions. He believed the game was played to be won, and he made sure we knew that every ball mattered. His lessons – on effort, on integrity, on resilience – remain with me to this day.

Mark's book is not just about the Ashes. It's about change – how a game adapts, how players grow, how culture shifts. He captures not just the facts, but the feeling of an era: the frustrations, the hopes, the near misses, and the triumphant resurgence. It's a reminder that sport doesn't exist in a vacuum. It reflects us. It challenges us. And sometimes, it redeems us.

If you're holding this book, you're holding a piece of that journey. The Ashes series of the 60s may not have always glittered, but they mattered. They mattered to the players who gave everything for their country. They mattered to the fans who still turned up, hoping for a spark. And they mattered to kids like me, who watched and listened and dreamed.

So here's to that decade – not forgotten, but finally understood. And here's to the Ashes: enduring, evolving, and forever essential.

– Greg Chappell

INTRODUCTION

The Ashes is Test cricket's enduring showpiece. The rivalry between Australia and England in the five-day format has never been greater, nor, despite the incessant negativity of some cricketing administrators, marketing men and players who should know better, has the enthusiastic following for a contest that began back in 1877.

Test cricket for the Ashes has stood the test of time better than any other cricketing contest whatever the format. But this tiny iconic Urn, which has inspired so much sweat and toil and so many words, was nearly thrown out with the rubbish 55 years ago.

So unfashionable and slow-paced was Ashes Test cricket in that era that crowds and general interest dwindled markedly.

Brilliant players thrilled crowds in other Tests. It was an era filled with stars and characters whose reputations endure to this day. Benaud, Dexter, Simpson, Cowdrey, McKenzie, Trueman; all brilliant charismatic cricketers.

Yet during this time there were genuine regular high-profile discussions that the only way to rekindle the urgency in Anglo-Australian cricket was to ditch the Ashes as a trophy and concept. Prominent players, journalists and administrators debated whether The Urn should be killed off as the symbol of cricketing supremacy between the two sides.

What was the problem with the Ashes in the 1960s and how did it emerge from it's comatose slumber?

Here is the story of the players of that time, how they saw the contests with their arch rivals, why the games sometimes had the pace of a 45rpm record going around the turntable at 33rpm and how that wonderful tradition was revived to put it on track to the sensational must-see sporting event it is once again today.

It is set against the background of the parallel story of a sharply changing western social culture and the rise and fall of the iconic pop/rock band of that amazing decade.

PROLOGUE

February 20th 1963

The young opener not eighteen months ago had been lauded as the next big thing in Australian cricket. Then, just 24 years old, he was rated a talent to sit alongside the greatest names ever to wear a baggy green cap.

His 30-year-old English opponent was at that very moment in the form of his life. He had never bowled so well before. With his drift and spin and pace variations he had emerged as his country's leading bowler on the toughest tour of all.

But what should have been a duel for the ages was being booed and abused as if the pair was spruiking an unpopular political policy. Disgusted fans were noisily storming out of the venue as if they had witnessed a lame stand-up comedian.

They could not have cared who was playing whom. To them this was not a sporting contest, it was public torture.

The opposing pair would walk off the old cricket ground, proud of their achievements but also confused at the dissatisfaction they had created amongst the unhappy patrons.

What had gone wrong?

August 16th 1972

There were not many people in the old ground that historic sixth day in the South London suburb of Kennington, but hundreds of thousands were glued to their television sets 17,000km away in the southern hemisphere. It was the climax of a long absorbing northern summer between two equally matched cricket teams.

The strongly built teddybear-like Aussie left-handed wicketkeeper batsman pushed the short-of-a-length delivery from the tall blond South African-born medium pacer to square-leg. The 24-year-old West Australian called his 25-year-old Victorian, fellow teacher-trained batting partner through for the winning single. The pair, one with a future in education and the other to become a legend of the game, galloped off the ground together. The young man from Perth swinging his bat in huge joyous circles nearly collected his adopted fans, a cluster of Caribbean born teenagers who had supported the tourists throughout the whole Test.

His touring team had levelled the series 2-2 after a Test match that BBC television commentator, former England off-spinner Jim Laker, called one of the best he had ever witnessed or played in. Six days of cut and thrust cricket that could not be bettered.

After a long, tough journey, the status of the contest between the two countries for the little ceramic Urn was back where it belonged, right at the top of the Test match tree.

CHAPTER ONE

BANG BANG MAXWELL'S SILVER HAMMER

The excitement and glory that is an Ashes series remains after more than 140 years of one of the greatest and most loved contests in world sport.

Tickets can be sold out months ahead for most days in Australia and England, except for the 100,000-capacity MCG.

Getting into an Ashes Test at Lord's for just one day costs 150 pounds and then you have to be lucky. In 2019 Edgbaston tickets were also over 100 pounds apiece for an adult and still the 'sold out' signs were put up months in advance. Lord's could be filled twice over, so sought-after is every seat on at least each of the first four days.

For thousands and thousands of fans from both countries attending an away Ashes Test is an essential bucket-list event.

In Melbourne on December 26th 2013 the first day of the 4th Test of a one-sided Ashes contest briefly broke the all-time official attendance for not only Test cricket, but all cricket matches, when 91,112 people filled that massive stadium. That was followed in 2017-18 by the second highest ever overall attendance at a five-match Ashes series.

That 4-0 Australian win now sits No.2 behind the 1936-37 series when Bradman was in his prime. Then, there had been no Test cricket in Australia for four years, there was no television and the home side won 3-2 after being 0-2 down.

While T20 challenges all other formats in popularity and the changing viewing habits away from terrestrial television effects ratings numbers, the Ashes remains as popular and buoyant as ever.

It shows a special resilience that the culture and history of this contest retains its status and value when so much of the crowded sports program upon completion of an event is now as instantly disposable as a fast-food burger-carton.

Often forgotten though is the fact that Anglo-Australian Test series appeared almost to be on its knees 50 years ago. It was even strongly mooted that the concept of winning or losing the Ashes should be discontinued.

It would have been easy enough to do. The Ashes Urn is a little thing made of ceramics.

One blow with a hammer and it could have been smashed to dust and forgotten. The way Lord's and MCC was run in those days it might have taken a week or so before anyone even noticed the little guy was missing.

Had the Ashes Urn been destroyed there would have been a few suspects as to who had done the job. Several prominent characters in the cricketing fraternity had designs on disposing of it over that period.

In the 1960s draw after draw, at a time when widespread introduction of television into most homes, the family car and popular music were becoming available to the general populace, changed people's recreational habits and cut attendances and interest to record low levels.

Forget the repetitive fun of the 'Mexican wave'. This was the era of boos and the incessant slow handclap.

Between the exciting Tests at Manchester in 1961 and Sydney almost a decade later Ashes cricket went like this; 27 Tests, 8 results 19 draws. That does not include the wet Melbourne Test in 1970-71 where the sole piece of action was a coin being tossed.

Commenting on television on a sports panel show in 2015 about a boring rugby State of Origin match, highly rated Australian cricket writer Gideon Haigh mentioned that the scrappy League match reminded him of Ashes cricket in the 1960s. In both contests the prestige stakes were so high no player was prepared play the game in an adventurous way that might entertain and succeed but also risk defeat.

When Simon Hughes wrote *Cricket's Greatest Rivalry – A History of the Ashes in 10 Matches* (Cassell Illustrated) in 2013, he was able to move smoothly from 1953 to 1974 with barely a cursory mention of the decades in between.

Anglo-Australian Test cricket, seemingly more about not losing than winning, was uncool and only for squares. No member of the Beatles was ever photographed in the crowd at an Ashes Test.

Nothing much that had its origins in 1877 was considered 'hip' or 'fab' in the culturally revolutionary 1960s. Test cricketers wore suits and had short-back-and-sides haircuts. The 'mods' believed cricket was controlled by crusty, port-stained 'establishment' men who, the stereotype said, had attitudes locked in the Victorian era.

Even in a cricketing sense the Ashes was old hat, or Old Urn, at least. The West Indies was the flavour of the decade in the 1960s. Australians loved the cricket they played in the 1960-61 series, and England was equally impressed by their vibrancy and success in 1963.

There were those in the press who were fearful and campaigned for brighter cricket. The "brighter brigade" John Clarke called them in his tour book covering the 1962-63 Ashes series, *The Challenge Renewed.*

Clarke points out the passion English chairman of selectors R.W.V. Robins had for lifting the tempo and the relevance of cricket, English cricket in particular.

Robins, a close friend of Sir Donald Bradman, was not scared to stand on a few toes. He announced he was prepared to concede the Ashes to Australia if the English team lost in the brave entertaining fashion the West Indies had shown in 1960-61.

Hindering Robins in his objectives in England was the fact that several of the summers in which he was most active in his brighter cricket quest, the English skies were at their most uncooperative. Also, whatever he thought, many at home wanted to possess the Ashes more than they wanted "bright" cricket. This was especially so as, unlike in recent decades, the English were unable to watch the cricket Down Under live either on television or in Australia itself. There was no Sky TV or Barmy Army in 1965.

Apart from John Lennon having a casual bowl at Michael Crawford in Spain while filming *How I Won the War*, the Fab Four never showed any interest in cricket in any era or format. Unlike other contemporary rock icons who love cricket, I have never found a cricketing reference in any Beatles recorded material or interviews, either as a group or a solo artist.

But if they had been fans they would have been fairly easy to spot at some venues in the outer, distinctive haircuts or not. The whole match at Manchester, a city a mere stone's throw from the

Beatles' hometown of Liverpool, in 1968 attracted just over 10,000 per day on average. Only half the number that had gone through the turnstiles at Old Trafford in 1964 came back four years later. By 1972, with local County side Lancashire dominating the new and increasingly popular Limited Overs competitions, the number was down to less than 8,000 per day.

In 1964 at Manchester over five days the patrons had witnessed just 18 wickets fall for 1271 runs at less than two-and-a-half runs per over. The individual triumphs of Bob Simpson and Ken Barrington who made 311 and 256 respectively in that match have gone down in cricket folklore as monumental achievements.

Statistically, and as models of technical excellence and endurance, they were wonderful innings. As far as being part of an entertaining sporting contest though, they were anathema.

Over 100,000 cricket fans went to that match. In my lifetime and in conversations with dozens of English cricket fans of suitable age who have remembered or attended, not one has ever proudly said, 'I was there to witness those two great innings.'

They might instead have enjoyed *A Hard Day's Night* at the local cinema, which came out just two weeks before the Manchester Test to rave reviews, a lot more than the cricket.

Gideon Haigh wrote in *The Summer Game* one spectator at the match overheard by Australian leg-spinner Rex Sellers had said, "If that's fooking Test cricket you can stick it up your fooking arse."

He might have been speaking for the entire 100,000.

Australia's reserve wicketkeeper on that tour, Barry Jarman, said he had no recollection of the match at all.

Simpson, exhibiting a stunning array of brilliant shots, had once taken 18 off the opening over of the then fastest bowler in the world, Wes Hall, at the MCG as Australia set off on the chase of the 258 they needed to win the 5th Test against the West Indies and the series 2-1 in February 1961.

Now he faced 743 balls, scoring less than 100 runs of his triple century in boundaries, causing a number of Macunians to totally blow a gasket in their frustration.

When Simpson was finally dismissed on the third morning and was taking his pads off on the players balcony a Lancastrian member called out, "Declare Simpson you bastard." To which Australian wicketkeeper Wally Grout replied forcefully, 'What about the Oval in 1938?' (When England scored 7/903)

Here, possibly, is one of the strongest pointers to the intense grim nature of the Ashes Tests of the whole period.

There was an attitude of 'stuff-em' that filtered through the almost entire populace of both countries, all the way up to the cricketers representing them.

Players who played before the Ian Chappell era consistently placed their hand on their heart and said they did not sledge. Many old-timers were aghast at Michael Clarke's expletive-laden comments to Jimmy Anderson about getting ready to have his effing arm broken by Mitchell Johnson in Brisbane in 2013.

Yet there was no shortage of ill-feeling and resentment between players and even teams in others eras as well.

This was a legacy of... well, where do you want to start? Bodyline? Bradman not walking at Brisbane in 1946? The Laker spin-friendly doctored wickets of 1956? The Trevor Bailey time wasting at Leeds in 1953? Fuserium, whatever that is, infecting the grass on the pitch at Leeds in 1972? The Aussie 'chuckers' in 1958-59? W.G. Grace running out the young pitch-gardening Sammy Jones at The Oval in 'THE' Ashes Test in 1882?

Some English players insisted they walked if they knew they had hit the ball. When they held their ground at the crease in Ashes Tests after edging the ball to the wicketkeeper Australian players thought they were being hypocritical. Then the Englishmen said they did not walk in Ashes Tests because the Australians always waited for the umpire's decision. In County cricket, they said they always walked, but not Tests against Australia.

This information tended to filter through after the event, however.

Egos clashed. Some grudges went deep.

Grout recalled Benaud and Dexter having harsh words with each other in the latter stages of the frustrating 5th Test of that 1962-63 series. Grout said Dexter went red in the neck and then was stumped next ball.

Dexter in an interview posted on YouTube in 2014 said he did not find captaining England difficult because he was used to it after captaining Cambridge and then Sussex before being appointed to captain his country.

But there is no doubt his end-of-season tension may have been compounded by the wear and tear on the English captain over the five-month tour of Australia.

Dexter had also led England on an eight-Test tour of the sub-continent in 1961-62 that lasted five months and he played the full 1962 season in England.

This was a good effort from a man not renowned for his ability to sustain focus on one target over an extended period.

He admitted in his autobiography, *Ted Dexter Declares*, "Perhaps I have too many interests, singleness of mind is lacking." Later in the same book he admitted 1962-63 was an "exhausting" series.

The pressure, intensity and expectation in Australia was sustained over the whole visit.

At such times what begins as a clear mind later becomes cluttered and distracted. It is no wonder Dexter's batting form and decision-making began to fray just slightly at the edges by the second half of February.

In a series of post-season Press articles, newly-retired, Neil Harvey was not very complimentary about Dexter's captaincy or relationship with the Australian team.

English writer Alan Ross labelled Harvey's articles "squalid" and "devoted to hysterical anecdote."

It wasn't the last time Harvey made prickly comments. Was this the real reason he was overlooked as a permanent captain of the Australian team?

In 2005 Fred Titmus wrote that Harvey's comments upset the English players "more than anything on the whole tour." All those years later the man who bowled brilliantly all that summer said he still could not understand what it was about. He did admit both men were "opposites".

Milan born, Dexter's father was an artillery officer in the First World War. His wife Susan, a model, attracted a wave of media attention when she arrived in Australia mid-tour.

Dexter himself also wrote of his tendency to irritate people with his intensity while playing sport, even as a seven-year-old at Primary (Prep) school.

Dexter was similarly chastised in a report from a prestigious English school. 'Lord Ted' did not emerge from the back streets of the inner working class Melbourne suburb of Fitzroy as did the cricketing Harveys. The English captain and Australian vice-captain paid each other few compliments.

Harvey fired the first salvo of a sequence of barbs at the English captain from Australian players in contemporary books that would have even made Kevin Pietersen look over his shoulder and drop his jaw. Dexter had a more restrained crack back at Harvey when he went into print.

In the case of each of the Australian captains in 1962-63, 1964, 1965-66 and 1968, one of their main claims to job satisfaction would be that they did not surrender the Ashes.

I interviewed Bob Simpson specifically about Peter Burge's famous innings in 1964 and generally about the 3rd Test at Leeds a couple of years previously.

When I asked him about the run rates he replied, "People weren't so worried about such things back then. They were more interested in the contest between bat and ball."

That was probably fair enough in a match such as the one at Leeds where the fortunes of both teams went up and down and the game reached a conclusion. It was less so in the next at Manchester and also in the 5th Test in 1964 where Bill Lawry after a laborious 94 copped the ire of Ian Wooldridge of the *Daily Mail* who labelled him "The Corpse With Pads On." Australia in their only innings in the match made 379 at 2.13 runs per over. The cricket was "mediocre" reported Leslie Smith in the 1965 *Wisden Almanack*.

The Australian batsmen had no method from which to score

with any momentum against the accurate off-spin of Titmus. At Leeds the 32-year-old Middlesex bowling all-rounder sent down 77 overs for 94 runs and at The Oval 42 overs for 51 runs.

"Titmus was one of the great off-spinners," Simpson says. "In my opinion the bowling then was far more accurate than it is today."

Fellow off-spinner Tom Veivers says, "Titmus bowled these drifters. They would hone in on the leg stump. And, yes, he was extremely accurate."

"In 1962-63 Freddie Titmus got me out in six out of eight innings," Brian Booth said, "But I did score some runs off him, so it was a good contest between Fred and myself. I did like batting against the spinners. He drifted out, but I thought he was an attacking type bowler.

"He flighted them up to you. He teased you a bit, but he bowled to his field and was an accurate bowler. I enjoyed the contest with all those fellows. It was a great privilege to play against bowlers of that quality."

Many players from that era are sensitive to any suggestion their approach was negative in comparison to the moderns. They are rightly proud of the fact that they were talented and dedicated enough to reach the pinnacle of the game. And they reflected the tenor of the times. A strong argument could be made in their favour that the teams of the 1960s would have the better of those taking the field 60 years later.

It is sad their numbers are declining. Opportunities to give their point of view on their era are diminishing.

The much loved of the Australians in the early sixties, captain Richie Benaud, passed away in 2015 from skin cancer. Brian Booth revealed that was one of several significant health problems for himself and his cricketing colleagues.

"My father and his generation, you saw in photos, they all wore hats," Booth says. "Our generation tended not to and I think we've paid the penalty for not doing that. I always wore a cap when I batted and fielded, but they don't give you that much protection from the sun. The floppy white hat was a better way of doing that.

"I know a number of players of my generation who have had cancers removed. I have had them removed too, from my face, arms and legs. And of course when we went swimming we were also unprotected from the sun.

"Smoking was more widespread then as well, and again my generation is now paying a penalty."

The destiny of the Ashes was a deeply rooted institution even as long ago as the 1960s with a rich and at times grim 80-year-old history.

In a sporting sense there was an enormous amount of national pride at stake as to whoever was deemed to 'hold' the little Urn. Defeat caused by some frivolous approach to a Test could be considered grounds for banishment either from England or Australia.

The late Geoff Pullar when asked about attritional run-rates in the 1962-63 Ashes series said to me in 2002 that it was caused by the field placings and the longer overs in Australia. The Lancastrian left-handed opening bat, who had a difficult time against left-arm swing maestro Alan Davidson, insisted that for both sides there was always a third man and a fine leg in position to turn what might be an edged or glanced four today into a single.

Genial Noddy Pullar, who also said a knee injury that was so bad by the end of the tour his room mate Brian Statham had to help him up the stairs at their hotel accommodation, suggested that from the longer eight-ball overs in Australia the last two balls were always played defensively. This was so that concentration could be maintained as the English batting rhythm was fixed to six-ball overs.

One fairly obvious factor watching old black-and-white footage of those matches is that few players came forward and drive the fast bowlers.

Another technical aspect apparent is that the backlifts of opening batsmen are very short, especially against the new-ball. And the first movement of almost every batsman to fast bowlers is back and across to the off stump. It is a method that works but restricts the number of front foot shots any batsman can make.

And at times not many loose deliveries were on offer from the quicks, either.

Brian Booth revealed the accuracy of English pace pair, Trueman and Brian Statham.

"Because of their age, they may have been a little bit past their best, but they all knew their trade. In Adelaide I was batting with Neil Harvey for a little while," Brain Booth says. "He walked up the pitch and he said, 'Brian if you are waiting for Statham to bowl you a bad ball, forget it. He never does'."

Back and across was an understandable technique. With helmets a decade or more away, a player forward-thrusting his forehead was a large target for the likes of 85-90 mph speed merchants such as Graham McKenzie or Freddie Trueman.

There was still a bit of backfoot dragging going on, too, so the fast bowlers did not always bowl from exactly 22 yards.

Also, a number of the fast men in that era ran in at such an oblique angle to the wicket that the batsmen only saw the last few strides if they looked straight up the wicket.

Trueman ran in from somewhere around mid-off. David Brown, who toured Australia in 1965-66, ran on a curve at least a quarter of a circle if not more.

The 1962-63 series was widely slated as a big disappointment. E.M. Lyn Wellings, never one to hold back on strident opinions, wrote in the closing chapter of his book covering that tour: "On leaving Australia I am more despondent about the future of big cricket than I have ever been."

This was a series that promised much and delivered little. Dexter upon arrival in Australia had trumpeted his team's plan to play positive and attractive cricket. Then when the deciding 5th Test was a dirge he offered the excuse that it was caused by the fact that the two countries were playing for the Ashes: "Concentration on the Ashes puts a dampener on the series. The time comes when one side sets its mind on saving the Ashes.

"If there were no Ashes and each man were offered 1000 pounds to win, there would have been a definite result that day (i.e. the 5th day of the 5th Test)."

Tom Goodman said in *With the MCC in Australia 1962-63* that he believed the English captain was suggesting "that there should be some special distinction for winning a Test rather than just one award, the Ashes, for the series."

Dexter eventually said he was making a flippant joke. But this highly controversial sentiment re-appeared and was supported on a number of other telling occasions in the following years of the decade.

Despite his pessimism Wellings penned another tour book after the 1964 series, *Simpson's Australians.* His last tour book was one of four listed by Wisden covering that tour. There had been at least six based on the 1962-63 tour. Like the crowds, these institutions of cricketing literature appeared to be in terminal decline.

Only two titles were released to cover the 1965-66 tour, one for 1968, the quickly remaindered *The Australians In England 1968* by the then recently retired captain, Bob Simpson.

My dad bought my copy, which I still have, for 50 cents, new in the book department of Myers Bourke St store in Melbourne in 1969.

Jack Fingleton, a master of the genre, also planned to write a tour book about the 1968 series, but when so many tour matches were washed out throughout May he jettisoned the idea.

For Fingleton to even consider it was a leap of faith. The former opening batsman against Bodyline bowling wrote after the 1964 series, "It is a sad thing about England-Australia Test matches these days. Something has happened. Much of the old fire has gone out of them and it would not be a bad idea if the top weights of both countries could form themselves into a committee and thrash things out."

Ken Mackay called one of the chapters of his book, *Quest For the Ashes,* "That Miserable Urn."

At the completion of the 1970-71 series there were no titles on the horizon, although in 1972, R.S. Whitington's *Captain's*

Outrageous, which covered most aspects of that tour, quietly and briefly limped onto the shelves.

As suggested by the title, Whitington did not have a very good time watching in 1970-71. He made a point of saying how he agreed with Dexter's assertion that the Ashes should be dumped.

He also quoted an Australian cricket official as saying that he dreaded the opening of an Ashes series as they failed to provide the entertainment of one against South Africa or the West Indies.

Happily the tour book did not die. By 2025 it remained a usually viable thing and had been joined in the intervening years by the VHS video, the DVD and the internet to provide all the reminiscent moments any hardcore Anglo-Australian cricket fan could want, either in print or visuals.

The last surviving Bradman Invincible, Neil Harvey, who played Ashes Test cricket from 1948 to 1963, is always happy to offer his thoughts about modern cricket.

Harvey was filled with disdain after he witnessed 50 English boundaries on day one of the Lord's Test in 2009. He complained about the quality of the bowling and the increased size of the bats. He considered they devalued each shot and the balance and interest of the contest.

Harvey spoke from a position of strength as he was an attacking and attractive left-handed batsman himself, in 79 Tests.

It may have been a different matter for players involved in an actual match. But there would be very few sitting outside the boundary who would trade tickets for day one of the 5th Test in Sydney in 1962-63 (England 5/195 from 87 eight-ball overs) to the 2nd Test at Lord's in 2009 (England 6/364 from 90 overs).

When commentating on the run rates and lack of fours in 1964 compared to today Bob Simpson suggested that another major factor was that the boundaries at many grounds had been brought in 10-15 metres.

"Particularly in Australia," Simpson says "You had to hit the ball all the way to the fence to get four. There seems to be a feeling now that you have to hit lots of fours and sixes to entertain the public."

No one, old or young, would want to return to the type of contest served up even into the early 1970s. It could be soul destroying.

In the final session of fifth day of the MCG Ashes Test in 1971 as Geoff Boycott and John Edrich successfully sought the red ink that would give their Test batting averages a bit of a boost, hundreds of fans grabbed metal drink cans and banged them on fences, seats and against other cans in semi-unified frustration at the boredom of the spectacle presented as sporting entertainment in front of them.

England had been set 271 to win by Bill Lawry on a very hot final day in two sessions. Largely untroubled while reaching 0-161, Boycott and Edrich made 76 and 74 respectively without ever hinting they might accelerate towards a possible win.

It was hard to imagine that any of the army of protesters, young and old, inebriated and sober, would ever bother to come back to see Australia play England again.

Even the players were bored. Australian spinner John Gleeson, to at least add mild amusement to the situation, stuck his cap on the upraised hand of an umpire who was supervising the moving of a sightscreen.

Gleeson, actually, didn't come back. He never played another Test match in Australia.

Several reports said the can-clanking protest was done with beer cans. Many were, but just as many protesters were kids using soft-drink cans.

One 13-year-old boy was tempted to join in, but sitting with his dad in the top deck of the Southern Stand he feared such a move would lead to chastisement.

Even for this budding enthusiast the cricket was hard going, however.

He had attended four days of this Ashes Test. It was historically re-scheduled after the earlier New Year's MCG Test had been washed out. By then the narrow wooden backs to the seats in the top deck of the old Southern Stand at the MCG, installed in 1937, had etched a significant and uncomfortable groove into the boy's back.

He was agitated, hot and thirsty. This was his proper entry level Anglo-Australian Test. Would he return again, or had an impressionable cricket fan been lost because of the tedious level to which Ashes Test cricket had sunk?

CHAPTER TWO

BOWL THE QUICK NOT THE SPINNER

In his last published work before his death in 1996, *Captains Of The Game,* famous ABC radio commentator Alan McGilvray wrote, "Bob Simpson and Bill Lawry fell in this restless period in which fighting, defensive cricket was equated with dull cricket."

He echoed the sentiments of much of the media to the cricket of that period.

McGilvray commented on Simpson's 311, "That (retaining the Ashes) was Simpson's great mission and achieving it seemed to transcend any peripheral activities, such as providing entertainment or providing public support."

This is supported by the summaries of various other journalists in the tour books published after each Ashes series.

The players, though, usually had a different perspective. It is not surprising that most of them backed up the various captains and their approach to winning the Ashes in the series between 1962 and 1971. For Australia Bob Simpson and Bill Lawry and for England Ted Dexter and Colin Cowdrey were gifted and successful batsmen. England captains in turn for the tours of Australia in 1965-66 and 1970-71, Mike Smith and Ray Illingworth were, respectively, an extremely popular man and a tough Ashes winning all-rounder.

Not all were totally enamoured with their leaders, though.

The late Neil Hawke in his autobiography, *Bowled Over,* was supportive of Bob Simpson's leadership. He was less impressed by Bill Lawry.

"As an on-field captain I had to place him at the bottom of my list. I cannot say my Test career came to an end because of Lawry, but it certainly was not helped," Hawke wrote.

Ashley Mallett, like Hawke a South Australian player, also had his problems with Lawry, but that was more to do with his lack of communication rather than his inability to force a win in Ashes Tests.

Lawry's fellow Victorian Ian Redpath was more supportive of his state and national captain. "Accusations that he was a defensive captain are fallacious," Redpath wrote in *Always Reddy.* Redpath explained Lawry's limited attack meant he had no other choice but be defensive: "Bill was as tactical as could possibly be with the material he had at his command."

Redpath suggests Lawry's approach would have been far different had Dennis Lillee and Jeff Thomson been at his disposal.

Lawry's vice-captain in 1968, Barry Jarman, had plenty of respect for his captain on that weather-truncated tour.

Jarman, another from South Australia, who for many years hosted his closest former teammates on his houseboat on the Murray River, was a patient wicketkeeping understudy for many years to Wally Grout. Eventually Grout retired in 1966, however, Jarman had only a couple of seasons as his country's number one gloveman before the demands of his sports equipment business took him away from the game in 1969.

He spoke to me shortly before he passed away in July 2020 at the age of 84.

"When he first came on the scene Bill was a dasher," Jarman said. "In a state 2nds match when we were both teenagers he belted us all over the place.

"And when he first came into the Australian team he was hooking and cutting and driving and scoring his runs at a fantastic rate.

"But as soon as he became captain that all went out the window. Obviously he put a lot of thought into what he had to do and I respect him for that. But he was a more defensive batsman for the most part after that.

"It seemed to me though, that Bill never thought any spinners could bowl. In England in 1968 he would ask me what I thought and I would say, 'Give Johnny Gleeson a go' and Bill would reply 'he can't get them out'.

"And to be fair to him I never had any trouble picking Gleeson's wrong 'un. Johnny said to me on the plane to New Zealand with the Australian B side in 1967, 'Come over here Barry and we'll talk about my signals to you for when I am going to bowl my wrong 'un and I just replied, 'Don't worry about it mate. You bowl 'em and I'll take 'em'."

Bob Simpson's 1964 side was one of several over the decades rated by the English Press as the "worst ever to leave Australia's shores."

But both Lawry and Simpson retained the Ashes in England. Would they have been better remembered if they had lost playing more aggressively? I wrote a story for the ABC Cricket Book in 2001 about the dread of being the captain who was in charge when Australia's Ashes dominance, which had started in 1989, finally ended. Eventually it was Ricky Ponting's 2005 side that surrendered the Urn in the most wonderful five-match series; the equal in quality and excitement of any modern sporting contest.

It was a marvel to watch and it would have been fantastic, exciting and nerve wracking to be involved. Everyone who participated could be proud of their contribution.

But would Ricky Ponting two decades later have swapped those garlands for another Australian drubbing of the old enemy like those that had preceded it for the previous 16 years?

You bet he would.

It is a huge gap in Ponting's CV that he captained Australia on two tours of England, 2005 and 2009, and lost the Ashes both times 1-2.

Richie Benaud on the other hand has a reputation as one of Australia's finest ever captains. Yet in that maligned 1962-63 series he should have received as much criticism as Dexter for safety-first tactics.

E.M. Wellings did not hold back. "The man praised for three years as the advocate and exponent of enterprising captaincy and cricket proved to be as cautious as the rest when put to the acid test," he wrote.

The series was tied at 1-1 when Benaud delayed his declaration on day five in the 4th Test in Adelaide, ostensibly because his main strike bowler, Alan Davidson, was injured. Then in the 5th Test he and his side declined Dexter's invitation to chase 241 on the final day in Sydney.

Benaud had let slip that he was unimpressed with Ted Dexter's captaincy and tactics as early in the tour as the Australian XI match in November. "I might have to alter my ideas," he suggested inferring that he too would tighten his approach to the Tests.

He called the final challenge set by his opposite number in the 5th Test, "a juvenile dare."

When asked about what happened during that Test, Geoff Pullar who did not play due to his knee injury, summed up the feelings of most when he said, "I think I talked to Sir Donald Bradman for most of the time throughout that match. I didn't take much notice of the actual game."

But he was reflective and supportive of the way Benaud and Dexter conducted the five games of cricket.

"You know what," Pullar said. "It was just the circumstances that developed over the series. It was no one's fault and no one was to blame."

In *Spin Me A Spinner* Benaud admitted the series had been a poor one. "The series as a whole, entertainment wise, was not a great success," he wrote without directly pointing a finger of blame at anyone.

His attitude to each contest may have been different if the West Indies had been his opponents. More importantly, he clearly did not want to risk tarnishing his captaincy record with a dreaded home series Ashes loss at the tail end of his career.

There could be an argument that the previous Ashes series in Australia in 1958-59 had been even more tedious. Then the run rates per over were even slower and only one six, hit by Trueman, a tailender, was struck for the entire series.

But home fans at least had the satisfaction of reclaiming the Ashes after five and a half years with four decisive wins. Four years later there were only two results from five starts and the grimmest of the draws was in that much anticipated winner-take-all, fifth Test.

Benaud's teammates remained faithful to their captain while

admitting that the 1962-63 series was a disappointment.

But over the next couple of years they queued up in print to take shots at Dexter for his part in the failure of that summer to stimulate the cricketing public.

In addition to Harvey's complaints immediately after the series and upon retirement at least four Aussies had a go at Lord Ted.

Alan Davidson, who had retired at the same time as Harvey, was the first in 1963 in his popular autobiography, *Fifteen Paces*. There was a balanced tone to Davidson's comments, but he was not afraid to point out Dexter's shortcomings.

"Dexter misjudged the character and capabilities of his own players," Davidson wrote of the English captain's broken pre-tour promise of brighter cricket. And of the problems in the 5th Test kicked off by England's sluggard day one progress after Dexter had won the toss and batted, "He overlooked the fact that time spent at the wicket is of no value unless runs are produced at the same time."

Ken Mackay left the Test scene at the same time as Davidson and Harvey. His book, *Slasher Opens Up*, came out twelve months after Davidson's effort.

He pointed to Dexter's defensive field settings based on the English side's proliferation of off-spinners. When Benaud responded with similarly defensive fields in the latter phase of the 5th Test Mackay said, "I do not blame him for employing a similar field to Dexter… He thought it time to retaliate in kind."

Then in his overall summary of the summer Dexter again cops it: "If England had been more venturesome early they might well have taken home the Ashes. Dexter must take most of the blame for their failure to do this."

Norm O'Neill, in the same year with the same publisher as Mackay, in *Ins and Outs* continued the theme of putting the blame on the other mob.

"On that first day (Sydney 5th Test), it was hard to exactly know what was going on. I know that we were mystified out there in the field. Neil Harvey was utterly bewildered and I suspect it was in that frame of mind that he started to prepare the articles which later incited so much comment," he wrote.

Wally Grout's *My Country's Keeper* came out a year later, from the same publisher. He was perhaps strongest in his criticism of Dexter of any Australian, outside Harvey.

"If Dexter ever writes his memoirs he would make a fortune by revealing his tactics for this Test (the 5th again)," Grout wrote. And in a more general line of trashing, "He can be a complete enigma-fired sometimes with inspirational qualities that can go as dead as a dodo. I still wonder if the team would have been more successful under Colin Cowdrey."

Grout prefaces these remarks by his wish that they will be seen as "constructive".

In certain circles within English cricket they were probably not seen in that light.

To this ex-school teacher a lot of these comments sound like a bunch of young boys blaming other boys at the end of a lunchtime spat.

Dexter waited until three years after the event before he replied to Harvey's comments. *Ted Dexter Declares* was released as late as 1966 and by a different publisher to the one that brought out the triple whammy efforts of Mackay, O'Neill and Grout.

Dexter relates that, "Harvey had announced his retirement after the tour and I had spent a pleasant evening with him and his wife and Benaud. I sat next to Harvey at dinner and listened to his plans for a new commercial venture.

"Harvey had been denied the right by the Cricket Board to write for the press prior to the series whereas his captain, a full-time journalist, was given permission. Some pent-up frustration may have built up in the great left-hander's mind. His retirement meant that he could release that emotion without fear of penalty.

"A few days later he attacked me at some length and in extraordinary fashion. I was 'the worst England captain I have met'. And 'seldom seen a prominent visitor to this country appear to be at times so ungracious to his hosts, the Australian team'. I drank champagne, 'but forgot to shake hands with the Australian team and say goodbye'."

This is getting close to territory that Michael Clarke and Jimmy Anderson would have understood half a century on. And there is the clear evidence of the harsh on-field words between Dexter and Benaud. Grout had a bit to say out there, as well.

But the tone of Dexter in his book is one of being perplexed at Harvey rather than to return fire.

Tom Graveney was an English teammate who later also questioned the wisdom of Dexter's tactics and decision to select him as the leader of the tour.

Not for the first time there had been indecision in England as to who should captain the side. Colin Cowdrey had been vice captain to Peter May and had stood in for the Surrey man in the West Indies in 1960, in the whole five Test series against South Africa in 1960 and at home in part of the Ashes series in 1961 when May had been slowly recovering from the effects of a serious operation.

The Rev David Sheppard temporarily returned to cricket in 1962 and was touted by many to take charge. Dexter had led the MCC on long arduous tours of India and Pakistan in 1961-62 and he was finally voted in.

His choice could never have been said to meet with universal approval.

One complaint was that with Dexter in charge, the Arundel-based Duke of Norfolk as manager and Sheppard as part of the leadership group, that the top end of the team was too Sussex-centric.

Dexter's captaincy reputation had, in fact, very much been influenced by one successful season as captain of Sussex in 1960. Wisden 1961 noted, "That Sussex accomplished the remarkably steep ascent from fifteenth place in the Championship table in 1959 to fourth last summer was due in no small measure to their new captain, Dexter, who proved a considerable inspiration to the side."

Even the vice-captain, Cowdrey, was from neighbouring Kent in the southeast. All that southern public school politeness and good manners was never going to receive the full blessing of the Northern contingent in the team. Yorkshireman Ray Illingworth in his discussion with Huw Tuberville in *The Toughest Tour* criticised what he saw as the selfishness of Colin Cowdrey in wanting certain positions in the batting order.

In Illingworth's own book, *Spinner's Wicket,* the then future captain blames "sharp words" he had with Cowdrey for regularly turning up late for nets in Australia for 50 pounds of his 1962-63 tour fee being withheld by the MCC. He said from that moment they never saw eye to eye. Indeed, to lower myself to referencing a County stereotype, most Yorkshiremen would not see eye to eye with anyone they believed caused them to lose 50 pounds.

Eight years later Illingworth was captain in Australia and Cowdrey remained vice-captain. Illingworth said he could not trust Cowdrey. The relationship was strained, although England did win the Ashes in convincing fashion.

Geoff Pullar said, "I don't think his (Dexter's) selection affected the team at all. He had been the skipper the previous winter so he was already in the job and we were comfortable with that."

But Graveney was less certain. In *Tom Graveney on Cricket*, he wrote, "I have said that Dexter was probably the best choice, but events proved otherwise.

"His handling of the field positions was often bad and the worst example was his use of David Sheppard."

And there was his choice of bowler at a critical juncture of the 3rd Test that Graveney believed changed the series.

"Dexter did a most peculiar thing in the third Test," Graveney wrote, "And it still ranks in my mind as the strangest decision I have seen on the field.

"(Barry) Shepherd came in for his first Test innings at the end of the second day with twenty minutes left. We had made a quick breakthrough and now needed to reinforce it.

"As I saw it the situation cried out for a burst from Brian Statham who had barely turned his arm over all day. Instead Dexter persisted with Barrington's leg-spinners in company with Titmus. The result was that Shepherd was let neatly off the hook."

Pullar also remembered the incident as what is now called one of the match's "big moments".

"When we were one up after Melbourne we should have gone on to win the Ashes," Pullar said. "Shepherd came in and he was very nervous. Statham was replaced by Barrington and went for 16 from an over. Shepherd was away, he played an important innings, they got a lead of 40 then Davo had this wild spell. We were 4-16 and the series was even.

"Richie (Benaud) would do all these crazy things and they would always come off. Norm O'Neill said to me, 'One day he will have to come unstuck', but he never did.

"Ted (Dexter) tried to copy Richie, but it would never come off. He just didn't quite have the same knack."

It was one of the Ashes greatest ironies that Dexter was criticised in 1962-63 for replacing a fast bowler with a spinner at a critical juncture.

Eighteen months later at Leeds he was again hauled over the coals after he replaced a spinner with a fast bowler at another "big moment" and again surrendered the initiative in the pivotal Test of an Ashes series.

Dexter was always nicknamed Lord Ted, but as captain in this case Unlucky Ted might have been a more suitable title.

His batting was along with West Indian Garry Sobers and South African Graeme Pollock the most dynamic and entertaining of the period. A number of his innings have become part of cricketing folklore.

One English writer said he was a great striker of the ball and not a great batsman. Another critic suggested he never played a match-winning innings against a highly-rated opponent.

These comments have about as much merit as the one made behind me in the MCG outer in the mid '80s when someone similarly suggested Allan Border was not that good because he only saved matches, never won them.

Both Dexter's and Border's doubters were way off the mark.

On a losing side at Manchester in 1961 Dexter made a stunning 76 before Richie Benaud turned the match in Australia's favour. He counterattacked the West Indians at Lord's in 1963, blasting fearsome fast bowlers Wes Hall and Charlie Griffiths with stunning drives.

And in the first half of the Australian tour in question he was in superb form with scores of 70, 99, 52 and 93 in his first four Test innings.

"He was a top class batsman," Brian Booth says. "I used to talk to Bill Lawry about him and we both agreed we loved the way he walked to the pitch twirling his bat as if he was ready to do business.

"Ted was a great strokemaker. He didn't just hit it hard. He was also a great timer of the ball."

His most impressive innings was a stunning 102 against an Australian XI at the MCG three weeks prior to the first Test, where he reached his century in even-time. England or MCC as they were titled in tour matches, on day one scored 5-458. A fortnight before the first Test he was practising what he preached. In *The Daily Telegraph* (UK) E.W. Swanton called his century a "tour de force". One straight hit, a skimming six off Tom Veivers' bowling is still rated as sweetly hit as any ever struck at the big Melbourne arena.

"He slaughtered me that day," Veivers says. "He belted me so much it delayed my Test debut by twelve months.

"I got him out at Leeds in 1964, caught behind square on the leg-side by Ian Redpath in close. And he turned and said to me just before he walked off, 'Well bowled, that squares things up', referring back to that match at the MCG in 1962-63.

"I've always thought that was a really nice thing for him to say.

"I don't want to comment on what problems Neil Harvey and he might have had. But I got on well with Ted Dexter. I got on well with him and found him to be a good bloke. I don't know what it was with some of the others. Whether it was to do with him being wealthy and from the upper class, I don't know."

Brian Booth, too, saw nothing to suggest Dexter was particularly disliked within the Australian camp.

"I was not conscious of anything detrimental as far as Ted was concerned," Booth says. "I had a lot of respect for him. Anything he might have been guilty of because of the staidness of that 5th Test I think had to be shared with other players, as well. But the game did go through a bit of a change there."

Ray Illingworth, a fellow off-spinner, wrote in *Spinners Wicket* of that shot against Veivers, "He (Dexter) struck the ball and though it rose no more than 10 to 15 feet it soared over the sightscreen and must have carried 150 yards. That was a fantastic shot that only Ted could have produced."

Ted Dexter was the handsome, charismatic, enigmatic superstar batting attraction of the era. A product of privileged colonial England, a long-gone era, it is hard to find a modern equivalent with which to compare him.

Later in the tour, between the fourth and fifth Tests, Sydney journalist Tom Goodman wrote that the attendance at the Victoria v MCC match in December was adversely affected because Dexter elected not to play.

Alan Davidson said he loved the intensity of the type of contest played in 1962-63 and that no one should complain just because it was bit slow.

Fred Titmus said they could not be played any other way.

But there is no denying the letdown everyone following the game felt when the 5th Test fizzled out.

The Cricketer magazine had previewed the 5th Test with the headline, "What More Could One Ask?" In the end the answer was a lot more.

Alan Ross was one of the great tour book writers. His final judgement at the conclusion of the 1962-63 series was that the players, in Ashes Tests at least, was losing some touch with the paying public if they thought they should be satisfied with what was provided for them.

CHAPTER THREE

1962-63 THE TESTS

This might sound like showing off or some sort of autistic spectrum behaviour tendency, but so familiar am I with the 1962-63 Ashes series, my actual match details below were first drafted off the top of my head and then checked back later with only a few alterations and missing gaps.

As previously mentioned, there were plenty of tour books covering 1962-63. All have some merit, the anticipation and controversies providing plenty of fuel for debate. My favourite is the smooth travelogue style of *Australia '63* by Alan Ross.

Now, in addition, there is the extensive visual record on the ABC's *Winds of Change: Cricket in the 60s* bonus dvd released in 2006. It was strange to have read several books covering the tour and then actually see hours of the action on my television screen. It was a relief that the footage matched most of what was written in the various tour books.

There are also a few precious minutes of colour footage on YouTube of a newsreel report of the 1st Test in Brisbane. To see the match, players and ground in 1962 in colour makes the coverage feel more contemporary. Then, the Gabba had a semi-rural look to it, in stark contrast to the deteriorating encircling concrete stadium of 2025.

So there on the screen is Barry Jarman in his first Test in Australia at the Gabba on a ground where he says he always had a lot of trouble with the crowd. "I was never their favourite," he admits.

That unpopularity would have been compounded when the South Australian dropped a sitter catch from Pullar off McKenzie's bowling in the first session on day five.

Jarman wore a white floppy sun hat rather than the baggy green which he seemed to prefer when later playing in England.

But it was not all grim and miserable. Games could be lost without players becoming completely downcast.

"At the end of the Melbourne Test England only needed four runs to win," Brian Booth said. "Richie Benaud called me over and said to me, 'Brian I am going to give you the great honour of bringing this match to a close'. So I came on to bowl. My first ball Colin Cowdrey played back along the pitch and said 'well bowled.'

"The second ball, which I thought was a better ball, he stroked me marvellously through the covers for four and that was the end of the Test match.

"We were disappointed to lose a Test match naturally enough, but I don't think it weighed on us too heavily because that was the second Test and we bounced back and won the third Test.

"So we knew you can lose one game and then you still have the chance to play better in the next Test."

1st Test

The Gabba Test that starts this journey was really a decent game of cricket.

After Richie Benaud won the toss and batted Australia fought back from an unpromising day one post-tea score of 6/194 to reach 404, thanks to a maiden Test hundred by Brian Booth (112). He received resolute support from Ken Mackay (86*).

"Two of my five Test centuries were in Brisbane," Brian Booth said. "I found the light nice and clear at the Gabba. It suited my eyes. And the pitch there in those days was somewhat similar to my home pitch at Hurstville Oval."

It would be the only 400-plus total of the entire summer from either side.

This was the first six hours per day, five-day Ashes Test played in Australia. Previously they had been six-day games of five hours per day.

Fred Trueman provided the first English thrust while Bob Simpson best thwarted his new-ball threat. The home side finished day one on 7/321.

Benaud had come in late on the first evening and he and Mackay added 91 for the eighth wicket before Barry Knight (3/65) cleaned up the last three batsmen and finished with the best bowling figures.

After English openers Pullar and Sheppard had added 62 then fell within three runs of each other, Dexter batted in the fashion of that stunning earlier MCG innings, making a powerful 70.

The captain's effort and hefty, if sedate, contributions from Barrington (78) and Parfitt (80) took England, who began day three at 4/169, to eventually within just 15 runs of the Australian total. Benaud (6/115) had re-asserted the dominance he had shown over the English batsmen in Australia four years previously. It was also a perfect follow-up to his devastating 7-18 against the tourists for NSW a couple of weeks before.

But the high scoring reduced the time his side had to set up a win. They rattled along on day four to reach 4/362. Lawry (98) and

Simpson (71) had an opening partnership of 136 and Harvey and O'Neill topped off the innings with aggressive half centuries.

Benaud declared overnight, but hampered by a sore ankle and a groin strain, he could not repeat his first innings success with the ball. Pullar and Sheppard made half centuries on a still flat wicket and although Dexter again batted superbly for 99, his openers occupied the crease for too long to make a last day target of 378 a chance.

There was a little flutter of excitement post-tea and the Australians believed they had one Englishman, renowned as a 'walker' caught behind, but he stayed and received a 'not out' call. In the end England finished on 6/278.

2nd Test

A match watched by nearly a quarter of a million people was won by England after a second innings burst of penetrative fast bowling by Fred Trueman swung a tight contest the way of the tourists.

The depth of the Australian batting lifted the home side to 316 after a middle order collapse against off-spinner Fred Titmus (4/43) and medium pacer Len Coldwell.

England on the back of a century by Colin Cowdrey (113) on his favourite Australian ground and another sparkling innings by Dexter (93) established a strong position at 3/254. Their lower order then succumbed to a superb spell by Alan Davidson (6/75) and they had to be satisfied with a lead of just 15.

Trueman (5/62) responded to Davidson's effort with some great new-ball overs. And with the bonus of running out Neil Harvey Australia slipped to 4/69.

Lawry dug in for his second half century of the match.

It became the first of his really obdurate Test knocks. On his home ground, the 25-year-old Victorian captain took 304 minutes to get 57. Brian Booth (103) made his second century of the series, but when a Dexter shooter bowled Lawry on the last ball before lunch on day four it broke the slow 92-run fifth wicket partnership and opened the door for Trueman with the second new-ball.

England needed 237 to win and when McKenzie had Pullar brilliantly caught behind down the leg-side by Jarman just before stumps it appeared England would have a tough task on day five.

The only wickets that eventually fell on that final day, though, were a couple of run-outs, one when the result was a formality.

Sheppard (113) followed a first innings duck and some unlucky fielding with a century that was the personal highlight of his two tours of Australia.

For some reason Davidson, McKenzie and Benaud could not draw out the vagaries of the pitch as successfully as had the English attack. A couple of catches were missed. Then Dexter (52) and Cowdrey (58*), completing a fine double soon after scoring 307 pre-Test against South Australia, saw England through to an emphatic seven-wicket victory.

3rd Test

As in Melbourne, a 2nd innings burst by a top quality and experienced fast bowler was the catalyst for his side's eventual victory.

In Sydney it was Alan Davidson not Fred Trueman who inflicted the decisive damage and Australia not England who cruised home by a substantial margin.

The home side just managed to squeeze in their win on day four before torrential rain flooded the SCG. Victory by eight wickets was nevertheless a just result.

Bob Simpson with scores of 91 and 34 not out, his best ever Test bowling figures (5/57) and some superb slips catching, would surely have challenged Davidson for Man of the Match honours if such a thing existed then.

Led by the still in-form Cowdrey (85), England passed 200 with only three wickets down. But they kept hitting Simpson's flighted variable leg-spin in the air to fieldsmen and were all out for 279.

Australia also built a position of strength on the back of Simpson and a chancy Harvey (64). They put on 160 for the second wicket before Titmus again caused a middle order collapse.

Australia was nine down and only one run in front when No.11 Colin Guest, in his only Test, joined fellow debutant Barry Shepherd. The pair added a precious 39.

With 40 runs in the bank Davidson (5/25) did his thing, swinging the ball in and pushing it away across the right-handers. Simpson caught three of the first four batsmen. England was four down before they had any runs in credit and 6/86 by stumps.

Injured wicketkeeper John Murray held on for 100 minutes into day four for just three runs. England was soon dismissed on the final morning for 104. Apart from the weather threat, Australia reached their 65-run target without serious difficulty.

4th Test

Rare rain interruptions in Adelaide, poor English fielding, an injury to Alan Davidson and a conservative declaration by Richie

Benaud condemned this Test to the second draw of the series.

Sloppy catching allowed Neil Harvey (154) to eventually return to his best form and his partnership with fellow century maker Norm O'Neill (100) off 194 for the fourth wicket was a stroke-filled foundation of Australia's competitive 393.

In a coincidence that sends cricket stat nuts into an ecstasy that is unaccountable to most members of the planet, that was an identical total to the one compiled by the West Indies in their first innings of the 4th Test at the exact same venue two years previous, almost to the day.

It will come as no surprise that Sir Frank Worrell's side made their runs at a crisp 3.32 per six balls rather than the Ashes-burdened Australians who got to their 393 at 2.85 runs per six balls.

This was nevertheless the second best run rate for a completed innings all series.

When England batted Davidson sent down just four overs before limping off with a torn right thigh muscle.

As there had been in Melbourne and Sydney, big crowds turned up at the Adelaide Oval despite the hot weather and the declining energy in the game.

The batting collapses were minor rather than major. Dexter and Barrington made sixties and, while the young Graham McKenzie (5-89) stepped up in Davidson's absence to lead the home attack, England's lower order was hard to shift. Titmus held it together with an unbeaten 59 while Trueman conducted the best big-hitting splurge of the summer. Benaud's leg spin, waning in penetration, was the main sufferer.

Australia's first innings lead was 62. Simpson (71) and Booth

(77) then ensured it was not wasted.

Benaud set Dexter's side 356 to win in two sessions. They were in some early trouble, however, and there was never a chance of either side getting anywhere near a result.

Ken Barrington made 132 not out of 4/223. By the end of the game, though, he was facing the bowling of Harvey and Lawry.

5th Test

A tremendous build-up ended in anti-climax with the crowd booing and slow hand-clapping the players. Both sides blamed the slow pitch, the slow outfield, the other team and the curse of the Ashes.

This was the match where that young opener (Lawry) and England's best bowler, (Titmus) had been centre stage when the crowd were so disgusted at game's end.

According to journalist and SCG historian, Phil Derriman, one spectator was so incensed by the lack of player energy, effort and attempt at reaching a result that he sued the New South Wales Cricket Association for a refund of his three pounds admission. Of course in Australia in 1963 he lost. Maybe in the USA half a century later he might have been awarded millions in damages from the court! After all, your honour, the poor fellow must have suffered incredibly severe personal anguish from his tedium.

England had to win to claim the series and the Urn. They took first use of the pitch and batted until just before tea on day two for 321. Barrington backed up his Adelaide ton with 101.

Australia was 3/74 at stumps on day two. Then O'Neill (73) and Burge (103) added 109. That stand and a lower order boost from

Benaud (57) took Australia towards 349 and a lead of 28. Titmus (5/103) yet again had been the main threat.

Australia was dismissed by lunchtime on day four. Time now was running out for Dexter's side. With Sheppard (68) and Cowdrey (53) making half centuries and Barrington (94) continuing his rich vein of form to the extent of topping the series run aggregates for both sides with 582, they reached 8/268 before Dexter declared at lunch on day five.

Australia needed 241 to win in even time. They hinted in the rooms they would consider it, but at 4/70 had an excuse to shut up shop. Lawry (45*) in cahoots with Burge (52*) again had to dig deep, so, deep he dug, and to the chorus of barracking and boos sent the 1962-63 Ashes series into the deepest grave. Australia finished 4/152.

At tea on the last day in the Tied Test against the West Indies Australia had been six wickets down chasing a similar target to the one in 1963 at the SCG. Then, Benaud said he was going for a win and the last session of that Test has become legendary. But the Ashes were not at stake, of course.

Neil Harvey took six catches in his final Test, and Alan Davidson claimed a wicket with his last ball in Test cricket.

Ken Mackay and Geoff Pullar had played the final Tests of their careers in the 4th Test in Adelaide.

CHAPTER FOUR

BOWL THE SPINNER NOT THE QUICK

The Australian players in the party for the 1964 tour of England had several advantages over those who had played in 1962-63.

One legacy of the most recent Ashes series was that expectations of brighter cricket had been dulled, literally. Australia's most recent Test series against South Africa had also finished 1-1, albeit with a great deal more positive batting on show.

Brian Booth against Trevor Goddard's South Africans had a tremendous series hitting two centuries, including a second one at his favourite Gabba, and averaging close to ninety. Bill Lawry also had a productive summer. In Melbourne he made exactly 100 more runs than in the second innings against England in the corresponding '62-63 Test (157). The Ashes burden gone, he thrilled his beloved Victorians driving, pulling and hooking with confidence. Lawry batted about the same length of time in both innings, five and a bit hours.

South Africa with emerging stars such as Eddie Barlow, Colin Bland, Peter Pollock (the only bowler on either side to average less than 30 runs per wicket) and the wonderful 20-year-old batting talent, Graeme Pollock, could with a little more confidence have won the series. When the South Africans won in Adelaide Pollock had pulverised the leg-spin of Benaud and Simpson to brilliant effect.

Over the same period of time, England had been mired in a much more negative contest with India on the sub-continent.

Battling health issues within the squad, they had held on for five draws. Some amazing bowling figures came out of these dreary cricket matches. Between them the English and Indian bowlers delivered 783 maidens. Sort of an anti-Bazball philosophy.

The Benaud v Dexter contest had been the first time any series in Australia had produced three draws. Bob Simpson and Trevor Goddard repeated the dose 12 months later.

But Dexter v Simpson would top their immediate predecessors in the no-result Ashes stakes when there were four draws in the 1964 series in England.

This was not unique. Both the 1926 and 1953 Ashes contests and been decided in favour of the home side 1-0 in five-match series.

And to be fair to the Australian and English captains of 1964 there was little they could do about the rain that fell on Trent Bridge and Lord's in June of that year.

"We lost a lot of time in that series and also in 1968," said Barry Jarman. "It would have made a helluva difference if they had done what they do now and make up time on ensuing days.

"And of course they didn't cover the wickets in England then, either."

Whatever the disappointments of previous series and the developing criticism of playing for the Ashes themselves, the build-up to 1964 was still big.

And many English spectators probably subconsciously recalled the excitement of the fluctuating 1961 Tests and anticipated some more of the same three years later.

But the big crowd at Trent Bridge on day one of the first Test in 1964 witnessed just 85 minutes cricket. It was cold and it was damp and Richie Benaud, now in the press box, was not in a generous mood.

He went to great lengths to slate the English authorities for leaving the wickets uncovered to the rain once a match had started, so reducing the amount of cricket the paying spectators would see.

Jack Fingleton in the June 19 1964 edition of *The Cricketer* backed Benaud to the hilt.

"Years ago here I could see no logic in leaving a pitch open to the weather and then making frantic efforts to mop it all up," he wrote.

"The main consideration is the spectator in this summer sport and I must say thousands of them got precious little for their hard cash at Nottingham."

In the same article he also made note of the happy relationship between the Australian and English camps during the match.

There appeared to be copious amounts of goodwill between the two teams and in the Press Box, he suggested.

But when it rained again at Lord's and the first and second days were lost completely, diminishing England's chances of winning that match, the series and hence the Ashes, the mood between the two camps became strained.

In the very next issue of the same magazine as the one Fingleton contributed to, Columnist Felix admitted, "There were brief exchanges in the Press during the Lord's Test match which were a reminder that a certain fundamental difference still exists between English cricket thinking and that of the rest of the world."

The dispute arose after the Board of Control contacted the Australian team manager in England, Ray Steele, and asked if in light of two days play being lost to rain an extra 30 minutes could be added to the subsequent three days to partially recover the lost time.

This, of course, in 2025, is standard practice in all Tests.

The Australians declined on the grounds that the tour playing regulations had already been agreed upon and that to change them in the middle of the match set a dangerous precedent.

Felix also commented, "It is hard for a loyal Australian to realise that the destination of the Ashes is of minor importance to those whose job it is to keep cricket flourishing and English cricket solvent."

Minor importance? Really?

But the criticism of the Australian response to the request was not universal. Both John Clarke of the *London Evening Standard* and E.M. Wellings in his tour book agreed with the Australian response that such changes could not be made mid-tour.

What the MCC should have done is spent more time looking at their drains.

During the scheduled second day at Lord's there was no actual rain. But the drains at NW8 had become blocked and the water from the rain on day one lingered all afternoon in front of the pavilion.

Apparently the plans for these drains could not be found. They were old drains. They blocked easily. They should have asked Bill Lawry where the drains were. He could have told them there was one right on a length creating a ridge after he batted for six hours on their wicket in the 1961 "ridge" Test. And as he had been trained as a plumber he might also have been able to fix them.

Peter Cook in the 1960s wrote a brilliantly funny sketch about a working-class father telling his educated middle-class son that he should seriously consider abandoning university and the professions and follow in his footsteps and spend his working life "down the drains."

A cricket fan, perhaps Cook was inspired to write his "drains" sketch by the events at Lord's on day two of the 1964 Ashes series.

"I remember the weather forecast on the television for the next day (day two) was for it to be 'brighter'," Tom Veivers says. "Then we turned up and we never bowled a ball. We spent the whole day in the dressing room laughing about that weather forecast."

"It is difficult in England if you get a run of bad weather like we did during the Trent Bridge and Lord's Tests in 1964," says Bob Simpson. "The whole momentum of the game is ruined. You get totally mucked up."

The poor weather had come at a most inopportune time in what was generally a fine summer in England. But the rain and the drains and some dogged batting from Ian Redpath meant that this Test like the one at Nottingham was a long way from being anywhere near reaching a result by the time five days was up.

The 23-year-old Victorian playing in his third ever Test on the last day of the match batted 60 overs for 36 runs. He did not add to his total for the final 53 minutes he spent at the crease.

Redpath's batting throughout his whole 67 Test career was often dogged, punctuated with flashes of dazzling aggression, but I never saw the man who was my hero display batting inertia of the kind he succumbed to at Lord's in 1964.

Dexter was pretty much in the clear of any serious criticism up to this point in the series.

He had resumed playing after taking a break from the recently concluded tour of India.

Dexter was not yet thirty and yet like Peter May before him, and some of the Australian players of the era, could not see much sense in playing cricket for too much longer.

Mike Smith had captained the English side on the eight-week tour of India in January and February 1964. The five Tests were played in a concentrated schedule similar to the modern era. Smith handled all the necessaries well with the exception of actually winning any matches.

He was popular with his team, sympathetic to their needs, stayed on the ground when others were dropping like nine pins from illness and scored 306 runs at an average of 51 for the series.

The cricket, as previously mentioned, was abysmal though.

One highlight was the bowling of Indian left-arm spinner, Bapu Nadkarni. In the first Test at Madras (Chennai) in England's first innings Nadkarni's figures were 32 overs 27 maidens 0 wickets for five runs.

He was on the way to topping the batting averages for India and bowling 213 overs in the series while conceding just 278 runs. So many overs, so many dots; thousands of them. The bowling section in the scorebooks must have ended up looking like braille.

There were plenty of English critics, though, who thought Smith did such a good job in difficult circumstances that he should succeed Dexter as captain for the Ashes series. Eventually Smith was not only not captain, he did not play in any of the Tests against Simpson's side.

When Dexter was returned to the leadership for the Trent Bridge Test it was not to universal acclaim. Wellings and Denzil Batchelor were two English writers who thought he was not a suitable leader.

Whatever his failings, this instability cannot have given Dexter confidence in his leadership.

Bob Simpson was considered a competent captain and is not rated with the Australian greats such as Monty Noble, Warwick Armstrong, Don Bradman, Richie Benaud, Ian Chappell and Mark Taylor.

The man with the most perfect, technically sound cut-shot I have ever seen has agreed to speak to me on a number of occasions. His knowledge and recall of the game was impeccable and his manner friendly. Another from the era of never being seen in public without a liberal amount of Californian Poppy oil grooming their hair, he was hard-working and in control.

Once when I asked Bill Lawry to recall some details of a Test match he played in, he said to me, "Ask Bobby (Simpson), he remembers everything from the games we played in far better than I do."

If he lacked some charismatic flair Simpson was still twice the perfect man to pull Australian cricket out of a jam. In 1977-78 with World Series Cricket challenging the traditional game, Simpson was recalled ten years after his retirement to lead the totally inexperienced new Australian Test team in a fantastic and successful home series against India and on a tough tour of the Caribbean.

Eight years later as Australia's first national cricket coach, working with the equally motivated Allan Border, he restored pride in the Test and ODI sides through instilling a diligent work ethic.

"There was a touch of Keith Miller about Richie's captaincy," Brian Booth says. "Richie was a wonderful captain, a great encourager. Because he played so much with us he had an influence on both Bob and myself.

"But they were different. Richie's approach was very strong in the bowling side of the situation; setting fields, that type of thing. Bob because of his strength in batting and concentration may have favoured that side of the game more.

"I remember Bob saying to me one day on the ground, 'Brian everyone should have the chance to captain a Test side one day, just to find out how hard it is.'

"It is not an easy task.

"But overall I would have to say both players captained the side well."

The 1964 Ashes tour would be Simpson's captaincy high point. His sides were defeated in the West Indies in 1965 and South Africa in 1966-67.

In South Africa he was possibly distracted by the lawsuit he was fighting over his comments in his book *Captain's Story*, on the legality of the bowling action of his former teammate Ian Meckiff. Frustrated by poor results and marginal umpiring decisions, Simpson spent a lot of time on-field arguing with South African umpire Hayward Kidson.

A member of the Australian side who praised Simpson's captaincy in 1964 called that whole South African tour a "disaster." He said Simpson was not in a fit state to lead the side against a strong South African team.

Despite this, he was still by almost 100 runs the best performed batsman in the team. His superb 153 at Cape Town set up Australia's only Test win of the tour.

Again though, away from the Ashes, there was no shortage of positive cricket and results on these two tours. The ten Tests in the Caribbean and South Africa saw seven games reach a conclusion. Unfortunately for Australia and Simpson the tourists only won two of them.

No one doubted Simpson was the best man for the job in 1964, though.

England on the other hand still seemed to be selecting their captains as a result of Parliamentary debate. They changed their cricketing leaders like economic policy promises.

The next MCC tour to South Africa in the northern winter of 1964-65 would again be led by Mike Smith. Initially Dexter devoted this period of time to running as a Conservative in the UK Elections. After failing to be elected, Dexter arrived on the Veldt and played in all five Tests in the side being led by Smith. His form was hardly compromised either, with his 172 in Johannesburg amongst the best innings of the summer.

The merry-go-round would continue a while yet. Although, it never quite reached the madness of 1988 when four different captaincy appointments were made over the English summer.

Kevin Pietersen caused some captaincy jiggery-pokery within the English side in 2008 and they have chopped and changed their leaders between formats right up to the present time. But since 1990 the line of succession in the English Test captaincy has been at least as stable as the House of Windsor.

Dexter had not yet been as prolific as in his two previous Ashes series when the teams reached Leeds all square in 1964. But he had played the best innings of the Trent Bridge Test and after winning the toss at Headingley he top scored for England with 66.

His side though were bowled out for 268. At that stage it was the highest total of the series where the initial prediction had been that the batting of both sides was stronger than the bowling.

That total then looked very competitive when Australia slipped to 7/178.

The tourists had slumped to that position after being 1/124. Lawry was run out then the Australian middle-order struggled against the left-arm spin of Norman Gifford and that man, Titmus.

But nine runs after Neil Hawke joined Peter Burge at the crease, Dexter took the new-ball and brought his fast bowlers, Fred Trueman and Jack Flavell back into the attack in an attempt to quickly dispose of the Australian tailenders.

In the mid 1990s Peter Burge spoke to me briefly about his innings: "The new-ball had been due 12 or 13 overs before Dexter took it," he said. "I told Neil Hawke, 'we'll make the most of this.'

"I'd had nine years of trouble with Trueman. Now he was older and slower. In front of 20-30 thousand Yorkies, I got square. That added to the pleasure...."

Trueman bowled short at Burge and in his next four overs conceded 26 runs. He then blamed Dexter for not allowing him to place a fielder on the square leg boundary as he had requested. Those involved on the other side, though, thought Trueman's decision to use the middle of the pitch was a poor one.

Burge went on to 160 and had partnerships of 89 with Hawke and 105 the next morning with Wally Grout. Grout also punished more short bowling. When Trueman eventually did have Burge caught on the square leg boundary his reaction suggested a mood of 'I told you so.'

Australia took a first innings lead of 121.

The decision to take the new-ball was pilloried in the press the next day. Those writers compiling tour books and writing in *The Cricketer* with a little more time for reflection considered the decision to take the new-ball perfectly reasonable.

The consensus of that set of scribes was that Worcestershire's Jack Flavell and Trueman bowled really badly. The spell cost Trueman the next game at Manchester. Flavell never played for England again.

Dexter was criticised from all directions for delaying the return of the spinners for too long.

"Peter nailed it when Trueman came on," said his captain Bob Simpson in the 2013 interview. "He bowled too short and Peter was a beautiful hooker.

"Fred was a proud man and he did not like being treated like that, especially in front of his own Yorkshire crowd. He tried to bounce him and the shorter he bowled, the harder Peter lifted him into the square leg pickets and beyond."

Tom Veivers says, "Trueman bowled poorly. It was never Ted's fault."

England made 229 in the second innings and left Australia 109 to win. It took them 57 overs, but they got there with seven wickets in hand.

Simpson's side was one up with two to play. They were like a soccer team defending a one-nil lead. Everyone was a defender put behind the ball to protect the slender advantage. England never looked anything like scoring an equalising goal, let alone a winner.

"The side that we took to England in 1964," says Brian Booth, "was a different side to the one that went in 1961. We didn't have Benaud or Davidson or Harvey or Kenny Mackay.

"It was a changing of the guard, as it were."

"That label we got as the worst Australian side ever," Tom Veivers says, "made us more determined. It melded us together. Whatever way it is done to win the Ashes it is always a major achievement.

"We were a bit light on for fast bowling depth apart from Graham McKenzie. But overall we weren't a bad team."

Veivers admitted that at Manchester by late on day five the crowd were taking as much interest in whether he broke the record for the greatest amount of bowling in a Test match as to any thought of how the game might pan out.

"In the last hour of the match the crowd were cheering me," Veivers says. "They announced at the ground that I had broken Bill O'Reilly's record for the most deliveries in an Ashes Test and that I was close to breaking Sonny Ramadhin's record for the most deliveries in an innings in a Test.

"Even the England players wanted me to break Ramadhin's record. Wally Grout called out to the umpire, 'We are not going to appeal so don't give anyone out.'

"Then John Price, who has become a very good friend of mine, played over one and got bowled and I fell 17 balls short of the record."

Veivers bowled 95.1 overs during the English innings of 611. It was part of the 293.1 overs it took remove the ten Englishmen. Veivers finished with 3/155.

"Originally I was more of a batsman," Veivers says. "But I was told by Bill Brown and Sir Donald Bradman to develop my off-spin and to bowl tight. I had to bowl tight. They wanted me to go to England as a stock bowler.

"I was there in case the wickets were like they had been in 1956 when they were dusty and turned a mile and Laker did all the damage.

"And it was Jim Laker who did most to help me learn how to bowl in England. We went out for a meal together in a restaurant in London and he explained some things about bowling off-spin in England that helped me a lot.

"I got on well with and spoke to the Englishmen like Fred Titmus and David Allen about off-spin, too. But Laker helped me the most.

"But that wicket at Manchester was so flat. No one could do anything. There was no spin, no pace, nothing.

"It became a single innings battle. You just had to grind out the game, tough and hard.

"I admit it was totally different to today.

"But there are so many things that have changed.

"For me for a start there is the lbw rule. In those days if the ball pitched outside off-stump and turned back in, the batsman could stick his leg outside off-stump and pad the ball away and never be given out.

"And batsmen were just never given out if the ball hit the front pad then, either.

"Ken Barrington made 256 at Manchester and he was padding me away all the time."

Although Australia bowled England out on the first day at The Oval, that Test, too, was probably heading for a draw when rain brought down the curtain on the series 24 hours early.

"The funny thing about that tour," Veivers says "was that it rained during the Tests in the south of the country and was fine and dry when we played in the north. Usually it is meant to be the other way around."

So the 1964 Ashes series ended in an even bigger anti-climax than the series eighteen months before.

The postmortems were again unflattering and the Ashes Urn, or at least the overwrought national pride that gave them such eminence, got a lot of the blame.

Denzil Batchelor again raised the issue of ditching them.

"The Ashes *must not* (his italics) be the spoils of victory," Batchelor wrote, "as Dexter and Bert Oldfield have pointed out this season, as I pointed out in books and magazines after World War II, and as C.B. Fry pointed out from the time I first knew him.

"In simpler, ampler days men did not play cricket matches to retain anything (indeed they never thought about the Ashes), nor were they even imbued with the vital importance of winning a rubber.

"To them, the all-important thing was to win the game they happened to have embarked on."

Tom Veivers understands that the players' attitude to Test cricket was more dour in the 1960s to what it is today.

"The games were definitely played differently then," Veivers says. "In those days you won the toss and batted, made as many as possible and then tried to bowl out the opposition twice.

"At Manchester I didn't get in to bat until 20 minutes before lunch on day three.

"At the Oval I got 67 and managed to hit a few runs off Fred Titmus including a six, which I was pleased with.

"But these days they are supposed to complete a certain number of overs in a day. The big bats hit the ball like a wood hitting a golf ball. Neil Harvey reckons he could hit boundaries with the edge of the bats they use today."

Simpson's 1964 side lost to three counties as the tour of England reached its final stages. This occasionally happened to Australian teams as the fatigue factor of touring England for several months took some toll.

The 1964 team played a total of 36 matches, including eight after the conclusion of the fifth Test. Was it any wonder that their will to take cricketing risks diminished from the start of June to the middle of August?

And Simpson's side still could not go home after the completion of their fixtures in England. They then played in Scotland and Holland and they also had a tour of the Indian sub-continent tacked on in October.

The amount of money paid to the players and the standard of the accommodation provided in 1964 did not make the extra legs particularly attractive, either.

"I was away from home for seven months," Veivers says. "I think we got 2250 pounds for the trip plus expenses. It was a long hard tour.

"Then as soon as I got home from that I had to go off on a southern tour of Australia with the Queensland Sheffield Shield team.

"We stayed away from home for another couple of weeks while we played all the states in one long trip.

"I was working in radio for 4BC and trying to get a house built then. It meant that it was impossible for me to go to the West Indies in 1965."

Barry Jarman had three tours of England. He did not play a Test there until the third trip.

"I tell people I played over a hundred times for Australia," Jarman says. "But most of those games were against English Counties."

CHAPTER FIVE

1964 THE TESTS

Somewhere in the vaults of the BBC and the ABC there must be more film and video footage of the 1964 Ashes series in England.

But unlike its predecessor in 1962-63 there is not one lengthy moving document that has been made widely available.

There is some nice film coverage of England batting at Leeds in the BBC's VHS *Cricket in the 60s*. And in 2024 someone posted ball-by-ball footage of two sessions of the final day's play in the 5th Test at The Oval on YouTube. If you want an idea about why I think it is important to write this book, have a look at as much as you can of this dry old stuff. I usually can struggle through about three overs at a time at most.

In the film footage at Leeds, Dexter's 66 on day one features prominently and it confirms the awesome range and beauty of his strokeplay. The footage is film rather than live video and the dubbed-in commentator keeps referring to his shots as a "rasping drive" and a "rasping square cut".

Noticeable in the second innings of the same Test is Tom Veivers winning an lbw decision when Ken Barrington pads up to the ball near the end of day three. The Surrey man gives an incredulous look at umpire Fred Price, a former Test wicketkeeper from London rivals Middlesex, when he gives him out. It was the type of look that suggested he penned a letter to *The Times* in protest that very evening.

But Veivers is bowling around the wicket and the ball does

appear to pitch in line and turn back. DRS might have been interesting on that one.

On the same video there is coverage of Geoff Boycott's maiden Test hundred at the Oval and the often-repeated footage of Trueman claiming his 300th Test wicket.

Other snippets can be found of newsreel film of the truncated day one at Trent Bridge on a *Green Umbrella* DVD dedicated to the whole history of the Ashes and there is a nice colour report from British Pathe again, of the play on the last couple of days at Lord's. It's also available on YouTube.

1st Test

Rain ruined this Test. That included all of the third day being lost. The bad weather dampened everyone's enthusiasm after an enticing build up throughout a sunny May.

In the time available Geoff Boycott (48) made a promising Test debut, top scoring in England's 8/216dec. Dexter's declaration, not outlandish because of the time lost, was not made until the fourth morning of the match.

Australia on the damp pitch battled to 168 in 78 overs. Simpson's even half-century at No.6, an identical score to the one he compiled in the opening Test of the previous Ashes series, and Trueman's running out of Brian Booth from short leg for 0 were the isolated highlights.

"I jumped down the wicket to a flighted ball (from David Allen) to punch it into the gap at mid-wicket," Brian Booth says. "I just got to it on the full-toss but hit it a little bit off centre and the bat for some reason turned in the grip in the handle. And I didn't know where the ball had gone.

"I knew it hadn't gone where I wanted it to go. I was a yard or so out of my crease. Then I saw Freddie Trueman at short leg had the ball in his hand. I was transfixed for a moment and he popped the ball into the stumps and knocked them over, saying 'bad luck Brian' as he did so.

"But in my mind the cause was always that the rubber grip had become loose on the bat handle and the bat twisted in my hand.

"As Ian Chappell once said, 'when you're hot you're hot and when you're not, you're not'."

Off-spinner Titmus had opened the batting for England on day one when John Edrich was a late withdrawal an hour prior to the match starting, due to an ankle injury he suffered at fielding practice the previous evening.

Excuse me.

The injury was the previous evening, yet no replacement was available when he was declared unfit the next day. Nottingham is right in the middle of England. No County team, and there are lots of them each with at least two opening batsmen, could have been more than a couple of hours away.

Grout deliberately allowed Titmus to escape being run-out on day one after he was knocked over halfway down the wicket by the bowler, Neil Hawke. Hawke ran across the wicket to field the ball just on the on side of the pitch. His AFL credentials then came to the forefront as he gave Titmus an authentic hip and shoulder bump.

There was no question of ill intent, but Grout thought taking advantage would be inappropriate.

The generous Australian wicketkeeper therefore spared Boycott the first of what would be dozens of running-between-the-wicket embarrassments during his Test career.

In the English second innings on the fourth evening it was Dexter who joined Titmus against the new-ball and for a time he flayed the Australian attack.

The English captain hit 11 fours in 68 runs before being caught at cover on the fifth morning.

He declared again, the third time in as many innings against Australia, setting them 242. Calling his batsmen in at nine down was really a token because it was thought there was no point in the injured Boycott batting.

Simpson's leading fast bowler McKenzie had taken 5/53.

Australia's target was virtually identical to the one offered at the SCG 18 months before. It was required in three quarters of an hour less time, but the Australians had a go at it, briefly. After Norm O'Neill hit Trueman for four fours in as many balls then retired hurt after two blows on the same finger, it rained for the last, and most decisive, time in the match.

2nd Test

The Lord's Test was another total frustration and after two games it felt like the series had not properly got underway.

The early part of the match suffered more from the weather than even Trent Bridge. There was no cricket at all until day three.

England of course before 1930 had always played three-day Test matches at home. Most of them ended in draws.

When the cricket started Dexter won the toss and sent Australia in. They slipped to 6/88 before Tom Veivers (54) with the tail, doubled the total. Fred Trueman aged 33 and in his last Ashes series took 5/48.

Dexter opened the batting again, but was yorked second ball by McKenzie this time. Edrich, whose ankle had recovered, was one of three changes to the England side from Nottingham. The local selectors were up to their necks again in theories of balance and horses for courses.

But the 27-year-old opener from Norfolk's pre-eminent cricketing family made 120 in his Ashes debut in six and a quarter hours giving England a lead of 70. Young Australian swing bowler Graeme Corling took 4/60.

Australia began the last day on 1/49 in their second innings. Peter Burge (59) ensured they did not get into serious trouble. But if there were still any doubts at 4/168 twenty minutes after lunch, they were ended by yet more rain.

No rain had been forecast but unforeseen persistent heavy drizzle proved the Met Office wrong once again.

A young West Indian girl at the ground suggested to cricket writer Denzil Batchelor that England should give up cricket and concentrate on water polo.

3rd Test

It may not have been affected much by rain, however a cold wind blew through Headingley during the decisive Test of this rubber both figuratively and literally.

The real wind caused the spectators to rug up and the mood of the match to be a bit subdued.

The figurative wind was the sense that England had blown their chance to win the Ashes again as following defeat here, two wins would be needed to reclaim the Urn in the last two Tests.

On day one on a firm wicket England had the chance to assert themselves and missed out when they only made 268.

Apart from Dexter's previously mentioned 66 the best innings was by wicketkeeper Jim Parks, another Sussex man, who made 68.

Simpson's new-ball bowlers McKenzie (4/74) and Neil Hawke (5/75) took nine of the ten English wickets.

Day two saw Australia make a fine start through Bill Lawry (78) before England took charge as Titmus (4/69) choked off the run flow.

Australia, fighting hard, climbed back on top again through Burge (160).

They finished on 8/283 on day two, Burge having just completed his century.

"It was a magnificent innings by Peter and a big turning point in the match and for the whole team and lifted our confidence," said Brian Booth.

The tourists extended the total to 389 with Grout, like fellow tailender Hawke, making an important 37 on day three.

England in their second innings struggled to just 229, no one other than Barrington (85) going beyond 32.

On day four Australia claimed the last six English wickets for a further 72 runs before a young Ian Redpath (58*) guided a tense Australian side to what would be a series-deciding seven-wicket victory.

4th Test

A lot has already been written about this non-sporting contest in this book. Here is some more.

Lawry (106) and Simpson (311) added a then-record 201 for the first wicket against an England side that saw another four changes after the Headingley loss. They replaced the entire pace attack, including their long time new-ball spearhead, Fred Trueman.

Simpson's triple ton was his maiden Test century. As Australia piled up 8/656 Brian Booth (98), previously having scored just 38 runs for the series, also cashed in. He put on 219 for the fifth wicket with his captain. On debut, Tom Cartwright (2/118) sent down 77 overs in the Australian innings.

"I wasn't playing for a draw just to retain the Ashes, at all," Simpson says. "The plan was once we knew we were going well to get a big score and then bowl England out twice to win the game.

"I tried every match to bat as long as possible. But at that stage I had never made a Test century. I was really annoyed with myself. I had made all these first-class hundreds, so it was ridiculous that I had taken so long to get a Test century.

"I vowed when I got that hundred in a Test I would make it a big one.

"I soon realised the wicket was flat and that my batting judgment during the innings was impeccable so it was my big chance.

"It was hard to score quickly as the English bowlers, and this is a general comment, were very accurate. They didn't give you much. But in a way that could be a disadvantage as they were also very predictable.

"You knew what they were trying to do and where they would

land the ball, more than with some of the other attacks around the world.

"Of my two big centuries against England I look back at the 311 at Manchester as the most pleasing because I had waited since 1957-58 to get a Test 100 and then I turned it into something special."

Brian Booth, who was told by Simpson he was the best vice-captain he ever had, was much relieved to be out there and to get some runs.

"I was asked my opinion on the side for the fourth Test by Bob and the other tour selector, Peter Burge," Booth said. "I said, that maybe it was time I was left out because of my lack of runs in the first three Tests.

"They replied that they thought I might say that, but that they wanted me in and that I was not going to be left out. They said I had been playing well in the County matches and that so far in the Tests my luck just hadn't been in.

"That helped restore my confidence a bit and I was able to go out and put on that big partnership with Bob and follow it up with another 70-odd in the fifth Test.

"The wicket at Old Trafford unlike the one in 1956 did not deteriorate even on the fifth day. I remember when we finally declared Freddie Titmus pulled a white handkerchief out of his pocket and waved it around as if to say he was surrendering."

England quickly lost Edrich when they began their reply, but Boycott (58) steadied the ship with Dexter (174) who then added 246 with Barrington (256) for the third wicket.

Barrington also had a stand of 143 with Parks (60) for the fifth wicket. Veivers (3/155) sent down his Ashes record 95 overs, but the bowling honours went to McKenzie again (7/153).

In 2016 Joe Root got within two runs of Barrington's score in a Test against Pakistan at Manchester. It was close but the Surrey man's and Simpson's innings still remain the two highest individual Test totals at the venue more than half a century later.

England lost their last five wickets for 60. Australia had to bat two overs in their second innings to complete the match. They wouldn't have to now.

5th Test

This four-day Test (less 90 minutes lost on day one for bad light) was mainly notable for the recalled Fred Trueman becoming the first bowler to claim 300 Test wickets.

That event occurred on day three.

Cricketer magazine would attempt to get into the mood of the times when they featured Trueman on the front of the edition that covered the Oval Test. The caption under the photo said, "F.S. Trueman, We love him yeh, yeh, yeh." It was the closest the rampant 1964 Beatlemania got to having some recognition in mainstream conservative English cricket circles.

It was a good try, but it was a pity 'She Loves You' was already twelve months old and off the charts by then.

Before Trueman's flurry of wickets, England got into trouble by being dismissed on the first day for 182.

They had of course again made some more changes increasing the local players used in the series to 20 while Australia's side remained unchanged throughout the entire five Tests except when

Bob Cowper replaced the injured Norm O'Neill for just the 3rd Test at Leeds.

Neil Hawke (6/47) had swung and cut the ball beautifully in the England first innings.

By stumps on day two Australia had taken 123 overs to reach 5/245. That man Lawry (94) was the main culprit, ably assisted by Brian Booth (74), Veivers (67*) boosting the Australian total to 379.

England reached 2/132 on the third day then 4/381 at stumps on day four. Boycott (113) completed his maiden Test hundred and Colin Cowdrey (93*) returned to form.

Then it rained. A lot.

Unlike 1962-63 no big-name retirements were announced at the end of this series, although Graeme Corling, Australia's youngest player in the touring party, played his fifth and final Test at The Oval.

CHAPTER SIX

SHORT ON THE BACK AND SHORT ON THE SIDES

It is one of life's mysteries that Ashes cricket was often unattractive in the 1960s yet the Australian and English authorities scheduled one tour after another throughout the decade.

Leading cricket historian David Frith has repeatedly stated his unblinking love for Ashes contests. Even he struggled with the dour inconclusive nature of the games in this era, though.

He told me I was "brave" to try and write a book covering this difficult period.

"My unquestioning adoration of the game saw me through," he wrote to me. "In fact it was, in retrospect, a fairly enchanting era because there were so many mighty players on view, even if they didn't stir themselves all that much.

"They were unwittingly opening the way for a more urgent form of the game. We now see the consequences."

Distance of years does lend romantic attachment, covering over the many flat spots. But those in charge of the game were also lured, even at the time, because they scheduled another tour of Australia by the MCC three years after the previous disappointing series in 1962-63, with the 1964 letdown sandwiched in the middle.

It might seem obvious now that waiting eight years to bring back the West Indies after the brilliant 1960-61 series was ludicrous. But even then the various tours were usually planned years ahead. And the 1962-63 Ashes tour did attract a couple more thousand spectators than had the West Indies in 1960-61.

English authorities, to their credit, did bring the West Indies back in 1966 and 1969 after the fantastic 1963 series captured the imagination of the local sporting public.

The man in the street, they said, wanted the West Indies in Australia rather than the English side again. And despite the attendance of young Mark Browning at day two of the 5th Test the overall attendance for the series in 1965-66 was still down 140,000 (20%) on what it had been in 1962-63.

The previous home summer in 1964-65 had been of very limited attraction. Only one home Test, the first ever against Pakistan in Australia, had been played. The best attendance at the MCG had been a mere 14,035 on day two out of a grand total of 33,067 for the whole match. Boxing Day attracted 13,100 for the then traditional Victoria v NSW clash.

Yet it wasn't as if Melburnians were not keen to get outdoors or to the MCG. Crowds of 92,000, 93,000, 87,000 and 102,000 witnessed a gripping AFL/VFL finals series fought out between eventual premier Melbourne, Collingwood, Geelong and Essendon three months prior to the cricket Test.

And when the Beatles had visited Australia in June, while Simpson's side was fighting for retention of the Ashes in England, the crowds of well wishers in the streets of the city and outside their Southern Cross accommodation were measured in the hundreds of thousands.

I was one of them. Supporting my sister's teenage obsession we travelled as a family from Geelong to Melbourne and waited in Exhibition Street. When, to an almighty roar, the Fab Four appeared on the hotel balcony, I sat on my father's shoulders and waved as furiously as my little seven-year-old hand could go. I swear to this day George Harrison smiled and waved straight back at me, just me.

Likewise, there were an estimated 250,000 fans in Prince William Street in Adelaide as the Beatles stood on the town hall balcony and smiled and waved again in disbelief at mass adulation their image and music had created.

The Ashes was beginning to languish as a contest in the eyes of the sporting public. The downbeat mood prompted Sir Donald Bradman to appear at the Australian team dinner prior to the first Test and implore them to play entertaining cricket.

The previous time he attended the same function was before the 1960-61 tour by the West Indies.

"He told us he wanted us to get on top of their off-spinners," Brian Booth said. "And to move the game on a bit. They sensed the game might have getting bogged down a little bit."

In 1960-61 the game's authorities had been similarly worried and their plea had a wonderful result. For the 1965-66 Ashes series Bradman's big motivating speech resulted in at best muted success.

This time it would be Australia who had captaincy issues. Bob Simpson's position at the helm was not in question, but his health was. He missed two Tests through illness and injury.

Brian Booth replaced him. His form with the bat was so poor (average 16.8), though that he lost his place, handing the captaincy back to his fellow New South Welshman for the 4th Test. This stylish batsman, international hockey player and devout Christian had played for Australia's main side for the final time.

"It's hard to judge why things happen. I scored three centuries in a row in club cricket and got 80 for NSW in the tour match against England," Brian Booth says. "I think I did lose a little bit of confidence during the Tests though, and when you do that you try and play a little bit too hard.

"I found I was getting a start but not going on with it. I was getting to double figures and twenty but needed a fifty or sixty to stay in the side.

"Other factors might be going through your mind like your job situation or something. But I tried to take things one match at a time and sometimes it just doesn't work out for you.

"I came into Test cricket when I was 27 years old and was 33 when I went out, so in that sense I wasn't going to get better."

There was no equivalent immediate threat to England captain Mike Smith's position during this series. However, his batting average for the summer was barely improved on Booth's.

He had done enough as a batsman and captain throughout 1965 to be a certainty to lead England in Australia and in many ways his appointment was a success.

Smith wittily addressed the scepticism growing around Anglo-Australian Test cricket when he said in the early days of the tour at a reception in Perth, "I suppose we've come here to get back this miserable little Urn of dust."

In the end though, like those before him, he couldn't get his hands on the "miserable little Urn of dust" and eventually the series, in terms of results, followed a similar pattern to that witnessed three summers previous.

More than half a century on, 1965-66 is perhaps the most

difficult Ashes series in the 60s to get a real handle on.

The stats make it look like another in the long queue of underwhelming contests of the period. It's the one right in the middle of the decade that confirmed the trend of what had gone before and what would come next.

The lead up was hardly one sensation after another. Rothmans tobacco produced a pre-tour *Test Cricket Almanac* tour guide. There was so little to say about the upcoming series only three pages out of 68 were devoted to actual text. The rest was various records, flimsy pen pictures of the likely players and a flash colour advertisement for the cigarettes produced by the sponsor.

Even Ken Mackay, in *Quest for the Ashes* had an opening chapter that seemed to have difficulty finding an interesting lead into the actual tour and the first few paragraphs of Chapter Two contained the words "lukewarm", "dice loaded against it" and "not exactly inspiring."

Mackay's wry outlook and the ability of his ghost-writer Frank O'Callaghan to bring that quality to the forefront does still make this particular 60s Ashes tour book an easy read.

Once the series was underway there were few controversies. Smith was a polite easy-going educated Englishman who evoked sympathy for his poor batting form. Brian Booth could also cope easily with any diplomatic tasks.

The two sides were low in charismatic personalities. Dexter, a quality man with zany ideas at times, according to David Frith, was gone from the English side as was the loud-mouthed bustling "best fast bowler who ever breathed," Fred Trueman.

Dexter's other interests and a car misadventure resulting in a broken leg began his movement away from playing cricket. He would hit the headlines though, during the tour, with some of his ideas and assessments in his newspaper column.

For Australia, Doug Walters – eventually to become a national legend for his character almost as much as for his 5000 Test runs – stormed onto the scene as a brilliantly talented young cricketer. Not quite yet, however, the humorous phlegmatic darling of the SCG Hill he was to become.

Bob Simpson later wrote of how well the whole series was conducted, the minimal number of controversies and the wonderful relationship between the two sides. That too, though, indicated maybe it lacked a touch in the drama stakes.

He also praised the "attacking" nature of the cricket that was played. England took the dissatisfaction with the recent past seriously enough to appoint the MCC's Billy Griffith as tour manager. His remit was to oversee improvements in over rates and rates of runs per over.

The run rates in 1965-66 were faster than the recent past, yet the only meaningful occasion that it was sustained above three per (six-ball) over was throughout the Australian match-winning innings in the 4th Test. By comparison in 2013-14 there were 12 innings where the overall run rate for an innings was three runs or higher, and on several occasions it was more than four. In 2017-18 there were six innings higher than three per over and three others between 2.95 and 2.99. In 2021-22, the pandemic Ashes series, Australia never dropped below three runs per over an innings and topped four an over on the back of Travis Head's pyrotechnics. Even England, despite a 0-4 defeat, disorientation and discomfort, were around three per over, except when batting for a draw on day five in Adelaide and when embarrassing themselves against Scott Boland at the MCG.

The superior over rates of the period meant that on occasions during 1965-66 the magic figure of 300 runs was scored in a day, but there remained long periods of batting inactivity.

The way Walters launched his Test career and the series gave the batting momentum an early fillip. Tom Veivers said it was one of the highlights of his Test career to be at the other end as the 19-year-old tamed experienced off-spinners Titmus and David Allen with what would become his trademark nimble footwork, pull shots and on-driving. In 320 minutes Walters hit 155 including two sixes and eleven fours. But the Ashes rain curse of the 60s meant it was day four of the 1st Test before his innings was concluded.

"That was one of the two Tests I captained," said Brian Booth. "And I told Doug I was the best captain he ever had because I got him off to that 155 run start and he should never forget it.

"Seriously, though, he was 19 and he batted beautifully. It was a remarkable effort."

So, on consecutive England tours of Australia a one-all drawn series result only half satisfied everyone.

Simpson would not question the status of the Ashes, but he did suggest something could be done to break the deadlock.

"As an anti-climax to this tour there arose a great public debate," he wrote in *Captain's Story.* "Through Press, radio and television on the need for a decision in Test series… no amount of argument would reconcile opinion on this one way or another.

"I would support the idea of a deciding Test. Not a timeless Test."

Simpson advocated a match that lasted up to 36 hours, whatever the weather, but that it should not last more than eight days.

Fifty-five years later an eight-day Test would feel timeless, perhaps even endless.

The batting may have been more positive. However a major problem was that it was mostly far stronger than the bowling on show. Claiming 20 wickets in a game was again a difficult proposition.

Australia had totals of 8/543, 516, 6/443 and 426. England compiled 558, 488, and 9/485.

In addition to Walters' fine innings there were some other huge knocks. Bob Barber's 185 on day one in Sydney was his biggest moment as a Test batsman and set up England's win in the 3rd Test.

Like a number of his teammates Barber sported a severe crew-cut hairdo during this tour. Much more American than Anglo-Australian they were a throwback to the US Marine look of the 1950s and made the players wearing caps look like they did not have a hair on their head.

They had put their conversion to the prevailing fashions and looks of the Swinging Sixties on hold for a year or two yet.

Perhaps it was a practical choice and made the Englishmen feel cool in hot Australia.

Bill Lawry was scoring hundreds against this England attack in his sleep by the end of the summer. His 592 runs in the five Tests included three centuries. For Victoria, he scored 153 and 61 against the MCC and for a Combined XI in Hobart he made 47 and 126 not out against the same side. Overall the hook-nosed left-hander occupied the crease for 41 hours against the English attacks of 1965-66.

Lawry's total was the highest on either side. For England Ken Barrington and John Edrich compiled two centuries apiece, Cowdrey made yet another Melbourne Test ton and there was Barber's "purple patch."

Walters got two hundreds as well and Simpson and Burge one each.

The series was then crowned in the 5th Test by Bob Cowper's 12-hour, 307-run marathon. His innings in front of his home crowd lasted so long it spanned the change in Australian currency from pounds, shillings and pence to dollars and cents on the 14th of February 1966.

Not surprisingly there were a number of sufferers in the English attack. Titmus, perhaps having had his confidence knocked about by young Walters, was unable to repeat his success of four years before. He did have the consolation, however, of joining the run scoring festival.

David Brown and Jeff Jones, father of 2005 Ashes fast bowling/ reverse-swing hero Simon, proved promising if ultimately inadequate replacements for Trueman and Statham. At times Smith had to turn to the medium paced in-swing of a fresh faced, bespectacled Geoff Boycott in an attempt to break a partnership. Sensitive about his thinning pate and the sun's effect on it, Boycott turned back the clock to the days of Clarrie Grimmett by always bowling in his cap.

So serious was the controversial Yorkshireman about his first trip Downunder that legend has it on an immigration entry card he wrote "business" as the purpose of visit. Every other member of Smith's party allegedly had written down "cricket" in the same section.

Australia repeatedly changed their poorly-performing spinners throughout the series. In the pace department Neil Hawke exceeded expectations. Not much above medium pace with an action that looked a little uncoordinated, Hawkeye was nonetheless strong and accurate and could move the ball in the air and off the wicket.

Graham McKenzie, aged just 24, was rated a burnt out hack until he stormed back into form in the 4th Test. That was after originally being dropped then recalled!

England won by an innings in Sydney and lost by a similar margin in Adelaide.

The English Press blamed the late falling away of form of the tourists on the itinerary. They griped about too many easy up-country games between the 3rd and 4th Tests but contradicted that point by also saying that the team was too tired from too much hard cricket throughout the whole tour.

"We had a lot of cricket outside the Tests," Mike Smith said. "We saw lots of different parts of the country as well, with games in places like Mt Gambier, Bathurst and Moora.

"I found the most enjoyable part of the job was the cricket itself and your total involvement in it.

"I didn't like the lack of privacy, though, and the feeling you were living in a fishbowl all the time. That takes some getting used to."

Smith, like Dexter and May before him, partially overcame the "fishbowl" existence by flying out his wife and children for a period of time mid-tour. This, as it did on the previous occasions, brought about a bit of grumbling from the media. A few old time 'pros' in the team who could not afford the same personal luxury as their captain or disagreed with it on principal also had their say.

Those critics suggested it might have been a factor in the late tour decline in form. Did it sap Smith's strength?

"It was disappointing to be one up in the series with two to play and to be defeated so comprehensively in Adelaide," Smith said. "Australia made a number of changes from their side that was defeated in Sydney.

"Some were voluntary, some were enforced upon them. They all came off."

Smith's leadership remained popular within his team.

Jim Parks, wicketkeeper on several tours with Smith as captain, reflected the majority feeling of the players under him.

He told Huw Turbervill in *The Toughest Tour*, "Everyone liked MJK. He was a player's captain. I went to India, South Africa and Australia with him, and he was the shrewdest England captain I played under. It (Australia) was a super trip."

But Smith's lack of runs led to his place in the side being questioned. Then after a double batting failure and an England defeat in the first Test against the West Indies in his first Test back home in Manchester in June 1966, he was omitted.

"My own form in the Tests was just one of those things," Smith said. "But that was what eventually cost me the captaincy. Any player, captain or anyone, has to perform well enough to hold their place and I wasn't making enough runs."

What is interesting from this distance is that his team were prepared to be satisfied with his leadership when there was such a proliferation of draws with Smith at the helm.

The five-Test tour of India, previously mentioned, was a "draw-wash". In South Africa only the first Test reached a conclusion.

England won at Durban and then held on for four draws.

Back in England in 1965 an understrength New Zealand side was beaten three-nil, but a return three-match series with South Africa was lost one-nil with two draws.

After the tied series in Australia, England played three more draws in New Zealand. That was followed by the loss against the West Indies.

Leaving out the home series against New Zealand, Smith's overall captaincy record was two wins, three defeats and seventeen draws.

Modest, pleasant, with rimless spectacles, the impact of Smith's performances, results and personality on the cricketing public did not make a massive imprint. Compare the number of books written about Smith with every other post war English Ashes captain. He is a long way last in that regard.

His Australian counterpart, Bob Simpson, had a lot of time for his opposite number in 1965-66.

"Mike is a lovely man," Simpson says. "He had a good record, but not so much against Australia in Tests. But he was good to play against. He played it tough, but he tried to make a game of it by getting his side to bat aggressively.

"The truth is although the cricket was extremely competitive and that beating England was the greatest achievement any Australian cricketer could aspire to, I had a lot of close friends in the English side.

"The teams got on really well. I loved getting Ken Barrington out, but after play we would often go out to dinner together.

"We had played together in Ron Roberts International Cavaliers in South Africa in the early 60s and developed great friendships.

"Ted Dexter was also a helluva good bloke. He loved his cricket and he loved golf and I played with him a number of times. Over the years as a player and administrator he helped the game enormously.

"I wouldn't necessarily say the batting was stronger than the bowling that summer. What I would say, though, is that these were two teams of similar quality. These results were a reflection of the evenness of the players on both sides. You were never going to get a 5-0 or 4-0 result like we have seen in Australia in recent times."

The niceties between the two captains may have extended to one not wanting to nail the other to the floor in the 5th Test.

Needing to win, Smith allowed the English first innings to meander in the middle section of day two when the total was already past 400. The instruction to "hit out or get out" was obviously never relayed to the middle. In the end the last 30 runs were worth nothing.

Then on day five Simpson could have declared much earlier with the scores about equal. England would have been under pressure to set up a winning opportunity and would have potentially given Australia a chance to win which they might have used as an option or declined.

It seemed an honourable 1-1 drawn series too easily satisfied both, once day four in Melbourne had been washed out.

Simpson had other issues, although too many draws and his own form were not two of them.

After his team lost in the West Indies one of his leading batsmen, Norm O'Neill became embroiled in the controversy surrounding the bowling action of West Indian paceman Charlie Griffith and never played another Test for Australia. He was just 28.

There were further issues. The depth of his attack was very limited and the age and health of his wicketkeeper, Wally Grout, was a concern.

Then prior to the first Test he had his left wrist broken by Queensland fast bowler Peter Allan.

The injury took six weeks to heal. Simpson was fit for the 2nd Test and scored two fifties, but then missed the 3rd Test with chickenpox, of all things.

When he returned to the side in Adelaide for the 4th Test Australia was 0-1 down in the rubber and there was work to be done.

Just as his 311 in Manchester in 1964 effectively meant his side would retain the Ashes, his 225 in Adelaide in 1965-66, an altogether more positive innings, again ensured the Urn remained in Australian hands.

He and Bill Lawry broke their Manchester record stand of 201 with an opening partnership of 244. The pair took so many quick singles it drove Smith and his team to distraction. It set up a first innings lead of 275 and an eventual win by an innings and nine runs.

With Graham McKenzie ripping through England on day one and Colin Cowdrey getting embroiled in one of the few controversies of the summer, a run-out from a supposedly misheard call, England was easily beaten and the Ashes balance was restored.

Tired bowlers, a flat MCG wicket, rain and Bob Cowper's marathon ensured that balance was maintained until the end of the summer.

INTERLUDE No.1. An Early Test Debut

In the summer, my dad followed the 1965-66 Ashes series closely. I still have his copy of the yellow fronted 1965-66 *ABC Cricket Book* featuring Graham McKenzie's follow-through on the cover.

It was Douglas Browning who instilled the germ of my adoration of Test cricket. A very sweet gentle, unassertive devout Christian soul, he never pushed it but was more than happy for my cricketing passions to flourish.

I recall the news about Doug Walters' mighty debut century. He was young and successful, therefore instantly my favourite player. Then, later, I heard he had made a duck in Adelaide and I was shocked. But Australia had won that Test to level the series one-all.

Melbourne would host the decider. It would be big. Dad was going. I wanted to go, too. I was told it would be a long day. Perhaps too long for a young boy in grey short pants and not yet turned nine. I persisted and got my way. I was going to a Test match.

Maybe in retrospect it was 12 months too early. The only things I recall about the cricket were continually asking if England were still batting and when they finally declared, the roar when Simpson, after his double century in the previous Test, was bowled early on by a David Brown delivery that reportedly pitched middle and hit the top of his off stump.

There was enough space for me to move around a bit in the seats, but I was restless for much of the time.

I was disappointed. But my knowledge of the world was expanding. For example I learnt the difference that day between my beloved Chiko Roll and its far less appealing sibling the Spring Roll.

In fact, research suggests, the play on day two was more interesting than it was for the remainder of the match. As a contest the game slowly died out.

My hero back in that 1965-66 match, for one of the few times in his life, subdued his natural attacking instincts for the needs of the side and the sanctity of the Ashes.

Doug Walters did not get to the crease until day three. He then added 172 with Cowper for the 4th wicket, in the process making 60 in four hours. That man Titmus was there again, sending down 42 eight-ball overs for one very late wicket, while conceding just 86 runs.

The 20-year-old Walters also claimed the bowling honours for Australia with 4/53.

Day four was lost to rain and on day five, Bob Cowper copied his captain from eighteen months previous by shutting out any hopes of England regaining the Ashes with a broad-batted triple century.

As with Bob Simpson at Manchester 1964, Cowper's record was a statistical landmark, not great sporting entertainment. *Wisden* said it was a "quickly to be forgotten Test."

If *Wisden* forgot it, what hope did an eight-year-old have?

Well, I do recall snippets of my day outside the cricket. My first sighting of the MCG was awe-inspiring. I thought the giant sheer grey cliffs outside the ground that were the back of the 1956-built Olympic Stand were magnificent. Just out of grade three I didn't really use these words, however, the sub-gothic grandeur of the stadium impacted upon me. It still does. When the sun is out.

CHAPTER SEVEN

1965-66 THE TESTS

When digital television in Australia began there was for a while a fantastic program for sports nostalgia buffs on the ABC called *Late Night Legends.*

It showed all sorts of footage of historic events from a range of sports including cricket.

They did feature the 1965-66 Ashes series over one period of a few nights. But *Late Night Legends* mostly played in the wee small hours of the morning. As a working man who needed his sleep, I missed it and soon the program was discontinued.

'Robelinda' on YouTube extracted some segments, notably of Bill Lawry's three hundreds and, for some reason, the bowling of Ken Higgs in Brisbane.

It is still clearly film footage rather than video tape, but appears to have natural sound effects instead of the canned applause and crowd sounds of the previous ABC Test cricket films.

Lawry's batting lacks some elegance. His back lift has no Gower or Lara like flourish and perhaps because he was a pure left-hander he is bottom hand is dominant. He plays lots of pulls and tucks off the hip plus breakout cover drives.

Higgs, with a "I can bowl into my dotage" substantial posterior, who only played in Brisbane, is hardly Michael Holding or Allan Donald in style, either.

The BBC *The 60s* VHS also uses a bit of this original 1965-66 film. It is not much more than five minutes and it would be nice to have seen more of Bob Barber's legendary innings.

As previously mentioned, Ken Mackay and John Clarke wrote the tour books on this series. I have them on my shelves. Despite reading Mackay and dipping into Clarke, 1965-66 is still the only Ashes series in the 60s where I still feel I am writing about something I don't quite know.

1st Test

This was only the second Test played in Australia since February 1964, that token encounter with Pakistan at the MCG in December 1964 being the only other home Test. It is easily forgotten now that no Tests were played in Australia in the summers of 1961-62, 1966-67 and 1969-70. Did that mess with people's holiday plans or not? It certainly didn't freshen their interest in the game.

The first Test of the 1965-66 Ashes series was the second successive Gabba Test to be ruined by rain, the second Ashes Test in a row in Brisbane not to reach a conclusion and the fourth in a row at the ground not to have a winner.

It was an unlucky run as from 1936 to 1958 every Gabba Test finished. And of course a tie, as in the legendary match against the West Indies in 1960, is a result. There is just no actual winner.

Off-spinners, who had been such an influence in previous 60s Ashes series, had combined figures of 2-320 this time in Brisbane. These same bowlers (Allen, Titmus, Veivers and Cowper) suffered the majority of the big hits that saw eight sixes struck during the game. This was an 800% increase on the sixes in the whole of the 1958-59 series.

Still, there was no real likelihood of a result.

In scenes not dissimilar to the start of the 1964 Ashes series, rain limited play on day one to less than three hours and there was no play on day two.

"In 1964 three of the five Tests were badly affected by rain," says Brian Booth. "And this Test in 1965-66 that I captained in, was also badly affected by rain. So that accounts for four of the ten drawn Ashes Tests that I played in."

And even though there were moments of batting aggression the run rate still never got above three per six balls. Bill Lawry batted eight hours for his 166 and when England got into a spot of bother on day four Ken Barrington (53 in 187 minutes) and Titmus (60 in 160 minutes) put the "brighter cricket" decree on the backburner once again.

England did have to follow-on on the last day to which Geoff Boycott said, 'Thank you very much' and occupied the crease for an unbeaten 205 minutes to give the Gabba patrons the tamest ending to an Ashes Test they had ever seen.

The recent history between these two teams, the save-the-match sort of batting, the loss of play to rain and the absence through injury of key attractions such as Bob Simpson, Graham McKenzie and Colin Cowdrey made this one of hardest ever Ashes Tests to sell to the public.

Only Doug Walters' energetic (if spread out) debut 155 made it worth recording at all.

Walters didn't reach the crease until day three when Australia was in some bother at 4/125. The nineteen-year-old had believed he would be named 12th man, so he saw his selection as a bonus. In what would quickly become his trademark he hit his second ball from Fred Titmus straight down the ground for four. Even on debut he was more relaxed than most at the batting crease.

By the end of the third day, Walters, after spending 50 minutes in the 90s partly due to a delay caused by a runaway on-field canine, had 119 and the cricket world was hailing a new teenage batting hero from the line of Bradman and McCabe to name just two champions who preceded him from rural/provincial New South Wales.

While the innings had no eventual effect on reaching a result, what it did do was break the spell the English off-spinners had over Australia, in particular, Titmus.

In 1962-63 he had taken 21 wickets at 29.33. In 1964 he claimed 10 wickets at 30.1 and restricted scoring to 1.5 runs per six balls. But in 1965-66 he took just nine wickets at 57.44 and then later in Australia in 1974-75, seven wickets at 51.42.

It was not the sudden blast of runs that saw Shane Watson remove another English leading offie, Graeme Swann, from Test cricket in an hour one morning in Perth late in 2013, but Walters showed that English off-spin especially in Australian conditions could be tamed in relative comfort.

Two summers later he would also score prolifically from leading West Indian off-spinner Lance Gibbs.

Walters had taken a good look at Titmus and fellow English off-spinner David Allen in the lead up to his Test debut when he made 129 for NSW in the tour match at the SCG less than two weeks prior to the 1st Test.

"I admit I didn't have a lot of trouble with off-spin," Walters says, "tended to enjoy them actually. In Australia they usually didn't turn the ball much so that made it easier to face them, too.

"I tried to get down the wicket to the offies and get to them to drive the ball on the half-volley as often as I could. They often had a 7-2 on side field or in Australia perhaps 6-3.

"If I couldn't get down the track I would back away and try to cut them square into the off-side which had a lot of vacant spaces.

"Left-arm spinners who turned the ball away, such as Derek Underwood, were a different story though."

Walters' attitude to the off-spinners was the first small sign that this desperately needed attitudinal change in Ashes cricket had started.

"My natural game was that I didn't like to be pinned down," Walters says. "I always had a sense that the crowd liked to see runs scored. They would lose interest if the cricket was boring."

2nd Test

The weather in Melbourne gave this Test a chance of a result. Only one session was lost to rain.

But the flat wicket (would it have been given a "poor" rating today?), the dominance of bat over ball, the number of injured bowlers who were unavailable and a missed chance or two meant that it still joined all those games in the burgeoning Ashes land of the incomplete.

England, batting second, made a huge total, 558. Eight of the first nine batsmen scored between 41 and 109.

Colin Cowdrey, back in the side, played the most attractive innings, 104 in 187 balls. It was the third of three centuries he made at the MCG. Not one was a 'daddy 100' i.e. 150 plus, although two of them did contribute to wins.

The game also contained innings of 59 and 67 by the recovered Australian captain Bob Simpson, 88 and 78 by Bill Lawry, a 99 by another local boy Bob Cowper, 120 by Peter Burge, 115 by Doug Walters, and for England 109 by John Edrich and 71 by Jim Parks.

Boycott's first innings 51 occupied just an hour and a quarter.

The extra long boundaries on the MCG meant that although many batsmen showed positive intent, there were lots and lots of twos and threes scored rather than fours.

The centuries by Walters and Burge were compiled on the 5th day when Australia was 4-176 and still 24 runs in arrears with plenty of time remaining. Burge survived a stumping chance and the youngster and the veteran calmed things down with a fifth wicket stand of 198.

Walters joined an elite group, including the legend from the 1920s and 30s, Bill Ponsford, and current television commentator Greg Blewett, in making a century in each of his first two Ashes Tests. Despite many fine moments throughout his career, this amazing Test debut season in fact would prove to be Walters' best ever against England.

The final Australian lead was 226. England had two overs to get them. Rather than everyone shaking hands then packing up Boycott and Bob Barber actually had to go out and face the sixteen balls.

England was 221 runs short when stumps were drawn. Boycott had another not out to boost his average.

By the end of the Australian innings even Mike Smith was having a bowl. With due respect to a charming man, by then the game as a contest was a farce and the Test should have been terminated. Thank goodness in the modern era such a match like that 2017-18 MCG Ashes Test with a "poor" pitch, would be called off at an earlier point.

3rd Test

As they did three years previously, England grabbed a one-nil lead in an Ashes series in Australia with an impressive win.

This was a huge success for Mike Smith's side. They were in control of the Test virtually from the first ball before running out victors by an innings and 93 runs.

Unlike eight of the previous nine Ashes Tests, not only did this SCG game reach a conclusion, it finished on the fourth day.

Smith won an important toss, his Australian counterpart again being Brian Booth as Simpson recovered from his bout of chickenpox.

Surviving just one chance, Bob Barber and Geoff Boycott set up England's big first innings total of 488 with an opening stand of 234.

Undoubtedly Barber in making 185 played one of the great match-winning Ashes innings.

He hit 19 fours in less than five hours. Using a high-on-the-handle Gilchristian style grip he raced to his only Test century and well beyond.

Australia selected two wrist spinners, left-arm David Sincock and right-arm Peter Philpott.

This was a tactic used successfully with Shane Warne and Stuart MacGill on the same ground more than thirty years later.

On this occasion, though, it proved to be an expensive luxury. The combined figures of Philpott and Sincock were 2/184. Like their captain in this match, neither ever played another Test.

Neil Hawke (7/105) caused a middle order collapse with the second new-ball. But John Edrich at No.3 (103) held firm and the tail led by David Allen (50*) saw the tourists through to their big final total.

The wicket was expected to spin. However, it was English pacemen David Brown (5/63) and Jeff Jones who did the bulk of the damage against a flagging Australian batting line-up late on day two and into day three. The home side, with opener Graeme Thomas and first-wicket-down Bob Cowper making half centuries, reached a promising 1-81. They then slipped to 221 all out 267 behind.

Asked to follow-on, the home side fared even worse in the second innings. Off-spinners Titmus and Allen shared eight wickets, a threat for the only time all summer. Booth's side were all out for just 174, with ten wickets falling for 128.

Lou Rowan would later write in *Umpire's Story* that in Australia's first innings the Englishmen deliberately walked all over the wicket between overs to scuff it up for the spinners later. It is hard to believe such a tactic, if it was planned or even existed, made any difference to this result. Nor was it ever mentioned anywhere else.

4th Test

Australia's selectors reacted to the SCG disaster by making five changes.

Ian Chappell for his second Test and Keith Stackpole on debut joined Simpson in the side. Cowper despite a 99 and a 60 in his last two Tests was another on the sidelines for this match.

Fast bowler Graham McKenzie was also omitted for Queenslander Peter Allan. But Allan then pulled out with an injury and McKenzie was recalled. Allan never got another opportunity to play for Australia.

It gave the English another chance to emit their favourite cricketing cry, "Oh unlucky!" McKenzie proved to be a matchwinner with a six-wicket first day return.

"I was lucky to have Graham back in the side in Adelaide," Simpson says. "He did a fantastic job on that first day. He was a nice quiet almost shy bloke, but could be very aggressive, not with overuse of the bouncer, but in the right way with a cricket ball in his hand."

Sitting easily in the list of top five fast bowlers and top five best looking cricketers of the decade, McKenzie took 6/48 on day one as England were dismissed for a confidence-sapping 241.

Adding to the "unlucky England" flavour, Colin Cowdrey was run-out this day when he mistook a call of "watch the one" from Australian wicketkeeper Wally Grout, to be a call of "come one" by Ken Barrington. It was a strangely absent-minded reaction as none of the other 12 players on the ground or the two umpires were under the same illusion.

Simpson and Lawry then responded on day two with their impressive 244-run opening partnership.

Bill Lawry related how Simpson spoke to him as they put on their pads before they went out to open the innings in Adelaide: "Bill we've got to rattle them by going for anything that smells like a run. Nothing's too risky. We won't even call, just put our heads down and go."

There is a bit of footage of Lawry's innings on YouTube and some of the running does look like a tippety-run dare. In the hour before tea on the second day the pair added 80 runs to give Australia their momentum.

"I was also lucky to have Bill as a partner," Simpson told me. "We always ran lots of singles like that and had a great understanding.

"We could lay the ball off in just the position and at the right pace to guarantee there would be no danger in taking a run."

As an opening pair Lawry and Simpson were as good as any Australia has produced in 148 years of Test cricket and this crucial double century stand was perhaps their most influential in setting up an eventual victory and highlighted their talents most appropriately.

When Lawry, after hitting nine fours and a six, was out for 119 Simpson, despite illness, continued on to 225 in nine hours, ensuring Australia had a huge first innings lead of 275. During his first-ever century in any form of cricket at the Adelaide Oval, Simpson was restricted by the effects of a nasty gastric virus. He could confirm that issues and problems come in threes and must remember 1965-66 as his summer of incapacity.

No Australian has made a higher score in an Ashes Test in Adelaide since.

Barrington scored 102 in the English second innings and Titmus

53. But Neil Hawke in a golden period for the South Australian swing bowler claimed 5-54 and on the fourth day England had only mustered 266 for their 10 wickets.

The series scoreline leading into the final Test was exactly as it had been three years before, one-one.

5th Test

And exactly as it had been three years before, the final Ashes Test of the summer was a clunker that ended in the tamest of draws.

Smith rather than Simpson was ill this time. Did the Englishman not wash after shaking hands with his counterpart in Adelaide, or did the Australian captain breathe on the Englishman? Probably the bug was just doing its rounds.

There were a few excuses for this 5th Test having an anti-climactic finish and at least England's day one batting effort bore no resemblance to the corresponding match in 1963.

On both occasions England lost five wickets. On the first occasion they crawled to that head-shaking 195 runs from 87 eight-ball overs. In 1966 they made 312 from 78 eight-ball overs.

The standout batting star for the tourists was one of the villains of 1963, Ken Barrington. Whereas his recent Adelaide rear-guard hundred had lasted five and a half hours and only contained four boundaries, in Melbourne he belted his way to 115.

Barrington wrote that he was fatigued at the end of a long tour, dejected by the Adelaide result, believing even on day one of the 5th Test that they wouldn't and couldn't win the Ashes, and annoyed with the barracking he was getting from the MCG fans. His angry response was to slog a top-spinner from Keith Stackpole that ended up going for six into the Members Stand.

"Well that started it. I just couldn't go wrong," Barrington wrote. Popular, despite the barracking, the square-jawed Surrey man raced to his 100 in 122 balls, bringing up the ton with another straight six off Tom Veivers. This was not the first nor last time he would reach the coveted Test landmark in that way.

As entertaining as was Barrington's innings, his defeatism contrasts sharply with the self-belief in winning that Shane Warne displayed in the Australian dressing room before play on the 5th day of the Test that became known as "Amazing Adelaide" in 2006. There is no way that match, with both sides making 500-plus in their first innings, would have reached a conclusion if it had been played in the 1960s.

Later, Doug Walters (4/53) picked up a cluster of wickets, including Barrington caught behind down the leg side. Still, on the second morning, through Cowdrey and Parks, England continued to attack and reached 419 by lunch.

And then, as if to sum up the whole era and its slothful ooze towards anticlimax, the tourists who could only reclaim the Ashes with a win took their foot off the accelerator.

Titmus, to be harsh, one of the strongest symbols of the 60s stalemates, spent two hours for 42 when further aggression was needed. This did not delight the biggest crowd of the summer (68,000).

Sitting near the fence in front of the old Olympic Stand, young Mark Bronwing clearly was not the only one irritated by the inability of the players to move the game forward. Although I have no recollection of this, I have read that by mid-afternoon there was a big punch-up in the crowd in a certain infamous section of the Southern Stand of the MCG. No one from my family made any movement to join in. We were always a melee-reluctant group.

Half an hour prior to tea on day two Australia were batting in pursuit of 485. By tea on the fifth and final day the Australians were still at the crease.

England got the start they wanted when they reduced the home side to 2/36. But Bill Lawry extended his series aggregate to nearly 600 with 108 and Bob Cowper, on his home ground, compiled what is still the best ever Test score on the MCG by making 307. It took him 727 minutes to get there.

Lawry and Cowper batted most of day three. Their partnership was worth 212.

Walters also applied himself to survival. Entertainment and domination of the off-spinners jettisoned for the Ashes cause, he would eventually bat four hours for 60. At stumps on the third day Australia was 3/333. The Ashes seemingly safe.

English journalist John Clarke wrote of the gloom in the press box at the state of the game. These men had seen it all before.

Then to rub further salt into the wounded English hopes, day four was washed out.

Ten thousand very, very faithful fans attended the final day of the series. They saw their fellow Victorian, Cowper, resuming on 159 achieve a number of milestones. It was a monumental effort of concentration.

Don Bradman had told him after his Adelaide omission from the team that his fitness was questioned by the selectors. He certainly put that doubt to bed for all time.

But I can never forget as a teenager reading for the first time John Woodcock's match summary in the July 1971 edition of *The Cricketer* where he wrote about Pakistani Zaheer Abbas's 274 in the first Test at Edgbaston.

He said that Zaheer's marvellous innings was the highest ever against England apart those by Bradman, Cowper and Simpson's triple hundreds, but that neither of the two knocks by the Australians, both of which he witnessed, in 1964 and 1965-66, was a patch on the one played by the Pakistani, then in just his second Test.

Even a fine a writer such as Woodcock could be prone to lapse into an occasional English whinge. But there is no reason to suspect that this comparison of big totals by individuals was one of those occasions.

So the 1965-66 Ashes Test series had also ended in a whimper.

In addition to Brian Booth and Peter Philpott, Australia, other than an A tour of New Zealand, never again selected Peter Burge after this series, nor did Graeme Thomas make the Test eleven, although he did travel to South Africa in Simpson's touring side.

Wally Grout retired after the 5th Test. Sadly the iconic Queensland wicketkeeper, with the penchant for a serious flutter on the horses, had a bad heart and would be dead in less than three years.

Mike Smith after his omission in 1966 returned to Ashes contests for three more games (aged 39) as late as 1972. Modest Mike's run-returns were modest against Australia then, too.

Titmus had an even longer Ashes hiatus than Smith, not returning to the Anglo-Australian contests until late in 1974 when after a Caribbean boating accident his overall toe count was well down on ten. Jim Parks, David Allen because of age and Jeff Jones because of injury, were all finished as Test cricketers by the time Bill Lawry's squad arrived in England in 1968.

CHAPTER EIGHT

MORE GOLF THAN CRICKET

I have followed cricket in England so closely and visited the country so often in at least part of their summer that I know from just a mention of the year how good the weather was during the season.

This is a mostly useless skill to have, but there was a feature article in *Wisden Almanack* about it in 2000 and the summary of the levels of rain and sunshine each northern summer matched my own memory.

I didn't know whether to be pleased or fear how boring I might be.

My first trip to the northern hemisphere was in 1989. We saw no rain in England between the middle of May until the end of June. I wore shorts the whole time and sat in the sun. Australia had won two Tests by the time I had to return home. I had fallen in love.

The English summer had been similar in 1975 and 1976, and so it would be again in 1990, 2003 and 2006.

2000 on the other hand, while I was in England, was very wet. So, it was in a Browning non-visiting year, 1988. And 1968 when Bill Lawry brought his team over for the next Ashes instalment was a total shocker.

When Alan Connolly sold his 1968 Ashes tour baggy green Test cap at auction for $6,500 fifty years later, the rich green colouring was almost mint condition. The cap had had no sun to fade the colour and despite 553 overs bowling on tour it had been too cold for the sweat to soak in and take its diluting toll.

Doug Walters was rated as one of the great young Australian batting hopes of that team. After his Ashes success in 1965-66 he had missed the tour of South Africa the following summer because he was conscripted into National Service. Back in the Test side in 1967-68 against India, he scored consistently and had his average boosted by a couple of not-outs.

He arrived in England in April with a Test batting average of 83. It was significantly higher than had been that of Don Bradman when he, like Walters, turned up with that NSW country background and a slightly home spun technique in 1930.

Bradman began his tour with an innings of 236 against Worcester. Walters took several weeks and a number of innings to aggregate anywhere near that kind of a total.

"That 1968 tour was terrible weather-wise," Walters says. "Particularly in the early weeks we sat around day after day waiting for the ground to dry, playing cards.

"It was amazing though. We would sit there for hours. Then play would be abandoned for the day. Then in the late afternoon and evening the sun would come out and off we would go and play golf. We played plenty of golf, but hardly any cricket.

"It never worried me, because it was a seven-month tour, so we knew we would get some cricket in eventually."

Walters had serious difficulty in those early stages when he did get to the middle.

The traditional tour-opening County match at Worcester was completely obliterated by rain. Then in the lead up to the 1st Test Walters made 1, 5 not out, 7, 43, 61 not out, 4 and 34. That's 155 runs at an average of 31. Bradman in 1930 had made 236, 185 not out, 78, 9, 48 not out, 66, 4, 44, 252 not out, 32, 191, 35, 18, and 32 all prior to the 1st Test. That's 1,230 runs at 111.81.

1930 was not considered a dry summer, either.

Walters and Bradman were not really ever compared again. Which is probably much to the relief of Doug Walters.

"The wickets were wet all the time," Walters says. "Their spinners and medium pacers jagged it all over the place in a way I had never seen before and the wickets were slow. So much slower than anything I had seen in Australia."

That movement off the seam by quicker bowlers and the placement of several fieldsmen in the gully would haunt Walters on four tours of England where he never scored a Test century.

Almost the closest he would get to a ton over there was in the first Test he ever played in the country. With no significant form behind him and with Bill Lawry's team the rank outsiders, he batted at number four, higher than for most of his career, and helped set up what is still one of the great Ashes upset wins with scores of 81 and 86.

Manchester had hardly been hot and sunny, but it was dry enough to guarantee a result. That was fortunate for the Australians, because the rain returned with a vengeance at Lord's and Edgbaston.

England took the ascendancy throughout the 2nd and 3rd Tests. However, the rain blanked out so much time Australia made it to Leeds for the 4th Test with their 1-0 lead intact.

It meant a draw would once more secure the Ashes for the Australians.

A glance at the scoreboard suggests little out of the ordinary in the Ashes Test played at Headingley between July 25 and 30 in 1968. It merely joined the long line of unfinished matches.

Reflection, however, now indicates it may have been a watershed, in the Australian camp at least.

The scores were close; Australia made 315 and 312, England's first innings reached 302. The run rate per over was just above two throughout. In England's first innings it only got as high as 2.05 because last man Derek Underwood came in and whacked 45 at a run per ball.

On the last day, England needed 326 runs to stay in the hunt for the Ashes. All Australia had to do was prevent them from reaching that target and they would retain the little Urn.

It was totally in the nature of the era that in 84 overs England could only reach 4-230.

Australia had achieved their No.1 objective, but there were dissatisfied elements within the camp.

Several players believed a lead of 325 was quite sufficient to go for a win on day five. But the field settings and lack of faith by the proxy captain in lead spinner John Gleeson meant the first priority was keeping the England run rate well below their victory requirement.

The match already had a strange feel to it because Barry Jarman captained Australia and Tom Graveney led England. Usual captains, Bill Lawry (broken finger) and Colin Cowdrey (strained hamstring), were in the dressing room.

What should have been career highlights for both Jarman and Graveney were diminished in their eyes because of the pressure of the Ashes contest.

"After the match I was having a beer and talking to Tom Graveney," Jarman said. "And he told me, 'They ought to burn the Ashes.'

"I replied, 'You're joking.'

"But he said to me, 'No, I'm serious. If they weren't there we could play properly and have a real game of cricket and not have to worry about them'."

Jarman admits that not losing the match had been his first priority.

"My main objective was to avoid defeat, rather than winning," Jarman says. "To be honest it was an ordinary Test match."

Certain members of the Australian team felt that Jarman was following instructions from the dressing room on day five at Leeds.

"We felt Barry was being guided from the dressing room by Bill," says Doug Walters. "A number of us were disappointed. Most of us on the ground thought we should have gone for the win."

Ian Chappell was another who disagreed with the Australian safety-first tactics on day five.

He wrote in *Chappelli* of his reaction back in the dressing room straight after play in the day five Leeds stalemate, "If that's Test cricket you can stick it up your jumper. (Or 'up your ****ing arse' according to Gideon Haigh in *The Summer Game*) We didn't ever really try to win that. We could have beaten England and taken a 2-0 lead."

Editor Norman Preston who covered the tour in *Wisden* reported that the wicket was turning on day five. But Jarman used his main fast bowlers Graham McKenzie and Alan Connolly for 56 of the 84 overs. Lawry and Jarman had little faith in the spinners Gleeson and Cowper.

Cowper, who sent down just five overs, was asked by Ray Illingworth why he had not bowled from the Football Stand End of Headingley. In Australia's 2nd innings the Yorkshire off-spinner had bowled 51 overs and taken 6/87, his second best return in Test cricket.

"Don't ask me. Why didn't I bowl? It beats me," Cowper replied.

In *The Australians In England 1968* Bob Simpson's disappointment was expressed without any names being named.

"This had been a most disappointing day's cricket," Simpson wrote. "And the most upsetting aspect having been the reluctance of the Australians to go all out and try and sew up the series with a victory."

Simpson, this time, did not actually say anything about changing the structure of an Ashes series or ditching them. The highest run scorer in the series, John Edrich, was yet another Englishman who did, though.

He wrote in his autobiography *Runs In The Family*, "The Ashes, mythical though they are, ought to be placed on the shelf at the start of a Test series and unless won outright, left in abeyance until the next series.

"The final Test match on each of the last two MCC tours of Australia was marred by negative tactics. If the Ashes had to be won instead of just defended, much of that disappointment might have been avoided."

Illingworth, who had come into the side in the 3rd Test in the 1968 Ashes series and would in less than 12 months become captain, added his views on Lawry's leadership and on the events of the fifth day at Headingley.

"The Aussies tossed a great opportunity away by timidity off the field," Illingworth wrote. "You could not blame Barry Jarman. He was only interpreting the instructions and policies of his skipper."

In defence of Lawry it should be pointed out that on a grey, damp Monday fourth day his batsmen made only 191 runs in five hours. Was this under instruction, too? *Wisden* called the batting "dull".

Chief perpetrators of the day four dullness? Ian Chappell 81 in 228 balls and Doug Walters 56 in 184 balls.

Editor of *Wisden*, Norman Preston, was not a fan of any of Lawry's squad. Not one was selected as a Cricketer of the Year for the 1969 edition. This was and remains a very rare occurrence in a northern hemisphere Ashes summer,

Much of the pre-Leeds match publicity on the English side came from the recall of one Edward Dexter.

Were Lawry and Jarman fearful that here was the one man who could score a match winning 150 on day five on a wearing pitch? It would have been a big ask especially as the home side also had two nervous debutants, Keith Fletcher, who had a horror match, and Roger Prideaux in their line-up as well.

At the distance of 50 years it seems the prestige and glory of winning an Ashes series had been quite overtaken by the 4th Test at Leeds 1968 by the burden of the fear of losing them.

"When I came into the team in the 1960s both Bob (Simpson) and Bill (Lawry) did talk about the significance of the Ashes," Doug Walters says. "It was looked upon as THE series.

"But Captains on both sides were not adventurous. They would rather ensure they did not lose rather than go for a win."

After winning the first Test at Old Trafford, Lawry captained

Australia in 10 more Ashes Tests for nine draws and two losses. There was much more to him as a cricketer and captain than Ian Wooldridge's cruel "corpse with pads on" label. However, there is no doubt "Phanto" Lawry's playing career is as much defined by the stalemates he created rather than the games he won.

That same year (1968), those ne'er-do-well Beatles, now unshaven and with shoulder length hair, were adding nine-minute avant-garde noise tracks on side four of their self-titled double album in the all-white cover. That year they also played their groundbreaking bestselling seven-minute single 'Hey Jude' with an orchestra backing them on a prime-time top rating television program hosted by David Frost.

It is to be wondered how many of the 1968 touring side, one of the youngest, rawest and least-credentialed of all Australian teams sent to England, had a copy of Jimmy Hendrix's classic album, *Are You Experienced* in their music listening collection for the tour. My guess, none.

Tour bus recreation would have been cards, cards and more cards.

Most of the party of seventeen would have thought if someone was called "hippy" it meant they were a little overweight rather than a child of flower power.

Their major influence instead was Bill Lawry, whose image was of a haircut to satisfy any sergeant–major, his huge nose sticking out from under his baggy green cap and right over the ball, with no back lift, prodding delivery after delivery softly to the fieldsmen, hanging on desperately to his 1-0 lead.

He had said to Ian Chappell after the young South Australian's dressing room outburst at the conclusion of the Leeds Test, "We've done what we came here to do, and that was to win the Ashes."

That still meant a great deal to many people, however the numbers seriously caring continued to diminish.

Lawry might have been happy to retain the Ashes again, but Anglo-Australian cricket had now been bogged down for four consecutive series.

English fast bowler John Snow wrote, "It's hard to imagine a summer with the Australians visiting England as an anti-climax but that is exactly how I found 1968."

And he said during the Old Trafford Test, the same venue that had hosted one of the great all time Ashes Tests seven years previous, that Alan Knott had said to him, "It's hard to imagine this being a Test match."

"It was hard to disagree," Snow continued, "The sun was missing, so was the crowd. The lack of both meant there was no atmosphere at all over the five days."

Both young Englishmen were in their first ever Ashes Test. It reflected the view of the times that they initially saw the game as an anti-climax after having just returned from the sun-drenched, noisy Test grounds of the Caribbean.

There were four draws in that series, too, won 1-0 by England after a gift declaration by West Indies captain (later Sir) Garfield Sobers. But three of the draws did at least have a gripping finish.

Of significance far beyond any cricket match was the fifth Test at The Oval. This was not for cricket reasons so much as for its far-reaching political impact.

The game had an exciting finish and gave England some return for their dominance over the tourists post Old Trafford. However, it is better remembered for setting in motion the events that became known as the D'Oliveira Affair.

Although Australia entered this final Test of the tour one-up, not one batsman had made a century in the previous four Tests.

The closest scores to a century had been made by Geelong College pair Ian Redpath and Paul Sheahan. Redpath made 92 at Leeds and Sheahan in just his fifth Test and on debut against England, 88 at Manchester.

Redpath would eventually make two Test centuries against England. However, Sheahan, aged just 22 and with a gorgeous, elegant technique and initially considered a huge talent, would bat fifteen more times against England for a highest score of just 44 not out in 1972. That crucial innings which had a huge influence on the game's result would be the last time he ever batted against the old enemy.

Sheahan, like Walters, would admit to having a lot of difficulty finding a successful method against the medium paced left-arm spin of Derek Underwood.

"I was sort of conscious of not being good enough. If your confidence is not there you can struggle even more," says Sheahan. "I always had trouble with left arm round the wicket finger spin and Underwood used to bowl at slow medium pace. Not like a usual left-arm spinner, for example, Phil Tufnell. Underwood used to smack his lips when he saw me walking through the gate. He got me out far too often.

"I found out much later that you could play back to Underwood. I was generally a front-foot player. I didn't learn enough about how to play in England soon enough. If you played in England like you played in Australia in those conditions in 1968 it just didn't work.

"Your hands had to be softer. You had to let the ball come to you. You had to be prepared to play back a lot more to the spinners.

"I had to work that out for myself and it took me a bit longer than it should have.

"I didn't twig soon enough and in those days you sort of fended for yourself.

"If you pressed forward, pressed forward again he would rarely if ever give you a half volley and eventually you would just get an inside edge onto your pad and short leg would get you.

"In 1968, when the wickets were damp, he bowled more like a left-arm cutter than a left arm spinner.

"On that tour we always seemed to be playing with rain threatening. That is not conducive to results or entertaining cricket.

"Not that English crowds back then expected to be entertained so much. They liked entertainment of course, but in general they preferred an enthralling battle."

Redpath and Sheahan were two of five Victorians, along with Lawry, who were first choice selections for the Test side in England in 1968. Les Joslin, the youngest member in the touring party of seventeen and Team Manager, Bob Parish, were also Victorians.

When the fortunes of Lawry and the Australians deteriorated, as often happened in Australian cricket, the party split along state lines. There was no question of open disloyalty. Ian Chappell said that he thought Lawry tactically a better and more astute captain than Simpson. There was just a belief that there was a superior way to approach trying to win a Test match.

The weather was actually warm and sunny and the pitch flat when Colin Cowdrey won the toss and batted in the fifth Test at The Oval.

England made 494, by some distance the highest total of the summer.

Australia was therefore up against it again and Lawry responded by making 135 out of 324. He took more than seven hours and faced 401 deliveries to compile that score.

His teammates, whatever their feelings about their socially reserved skipper's tactics, never doubted his tenacity, that his heart was in the right place, or his ability to cope with Test match fast bowling. They respected the man and his position as captain of Australia.

He must have been so nervous about his side's durability. Time and the development of certain players would show it was not the weakest Australian side ever sent to England, though.

It did, however, have the worst performed batting tail in Australian Ashes history. In every innings apart from the first innings at The Oval the tail crumbled without even a whimper. Only on days three and four at Kennington was there any boost to the total from numbers seven to eleven.

The collapses in every other completed Australian innings went like this: Manchester 6 for 31 and 5 for 9; Lord's 7 for 32; Edgbaston 5 for 9; Headingley 4 for 8 and 5 for 31; and the second innings at The Oval, 5 for 15. No.11 Alan Connolly batted eight times in the series and made 5 runs.

Lawry's innings and the eventual last-minute win by England in the 5th Test were forgotten when Basil D'Oliveira, after making

158, was omitted from the MCC side selected to tour his native South Africa.

There was outrage at his omission. Many believed the MCC selectors had been nobbled by the Lord's conservative establishment and the proponents of the apartheid policy in South Africa. When Tom Cartwright pulled out of the side because of injury and D'Oliveira was brought in as a replacement South African Prime Minister Vorster declared that the all-rounder was an unsuitable selection and would not be welcome.

The tour was called off, the Anti-Apartheid movement grew in strength and South Africa's total sporting isolation became imminent.

CHAPTER NINE

1968 THE TESTS

The far reaches of my wasted memory space have stored the idea there was some sort of footage of day one of the 1st Test at Manchester from the 1968 tour being shown on an ABC Saturday afternoon TV sports program. It was about 30 minutes ball-by-ball coverage and finished before Australia lost any wickets.

I would say it was televised about a week after the actual event. I also recollect a few filmed news highlights on television news reports. Graham McKenzie dismissing John Edrich on the truncated day one at Lord's with a delivery that flew off a length and could have smashed him straight the face if he hadn't got a glove in the way is one strong image in my mind.

But, like 1964, the amount of actual footage for general viewing fifty-five years later is really limited. There's a neat seven-minute package on the aforementioned BBC VHS *Cricket in the 60s*, which has now been posted on YouTube.

It features a few thrilling shots from Colin Milburn's bullish 83 at Lord's, Brian Johnston getting positively orgasmic about Colin Cowdrey's slip catching as Australia are dismissed for 78, also in the Lord's Test, and nice coverage of the final day's drama at The Oval. There, Derek Underwood and dozens of English spectators just do enough to beat the rain and snatch England a victory five minutes before the series is due to be concluded.

Apart from another few seconds here and there on YouTube I have found nothing. Yet it must exist on BBC files somewhere, plus John Arlott narrated a colour film of the summer as there is a 15-second excerpt of Boycott being dismissed in the second innings of the first Test, also on YouTube.

And although the amount of press coverage was diminishing there were technological developments beginning that would within a few years help boost the profile of the game in general and Ashes matches in particular.

Bob Simpson's tour book only received moderate reviews. The match descriptions are nice and thorough, but it is certainly no *Brightly Fades the Don*.

What is noticeable, however, is the dust jacket. It features a bright green wicket and outfield in the close up of the action as John Gleeson plays a delivery with Alan Knott keeping up to the stumps. Colin Cowdrey and Tom Graveney are crouched in the slips.

I think it might be taken at Lord's. If so, Knott must have come up to the stumps to keep to Barry Knight as Gleeson did not face a spinner in that match.

I know of no other dust jacket photo of that type in colour prior to that release. There are tinted colour action photos and non-action proper colour, but none of the match in progress.

Edrich's *Runs In The Family* released in 1969 also has a dust jacket colour shot of him in action, this time at Old Trafford.

It must have been an expensive process to print photos in colour. This was still a nice small progression in the presentation of the game and a tiny indicator for the future.

1st Test

Australia had battled its way to 2/77 at lunch on day one at Old Trafford after Lawry won the toss.

Of that 77, the Australian captain reached a mostly passive 31. Then in the very first over after the resumption Lawry slog-swept young Surrey off-spinner Pat Pocock once for four and once for six over cow corner. The second ball went one bounce into the crowd, the fifth over the ropes on the full.

Out of the blue Lawry had given his side momentum and apart from one or two pin-prick challenges they retained an ascendancy that lasted until the match was won.

Lawry and Walters both made 81 and added 144 for the third wicket. When they fell within one run of each other to the part-time leg-spin of Bob Barber, Lawry hitting a rank long hop to mid-wicket, Ian Chappell and Paul Sheahan took control and put on 152 for the fifth wicket.

At the end of day one Australia was 4/319. England would find it almost impossible to win from there.

They did fight back well on day two. After Chappell was run-out following a misunderstanding with Sheahan the Australian innings quickly folded, six wickets going down for 31 runs. Then, chasing 357, Geoff Boycott and John Edrich slowly put on 60 before bad light and rain cut short the last session.

The obdurate pair continued their long-winded progress on day three extending their opening stand to 86 in three and a quarter hours.

It was Walters who gave the Australians their momentum back and woke up the crowd with a superb piece of fielding. A brilliantly accurate, hard and low throw from deep third man found Edrich short of his ground as he scrambled for his fifty. In an amazing statistical coincidence, the Surrey left-hander would also be dismissed run-out on 49 in the English first innings of the first Test of the 1972 Ashes series. That, too, was played at Old Trafford.

England then collapsed to 5/97, having out of nowhere lost 5/11. Their middle order totally crumbled to the pace of Graham McKenzie and the off-spin of Bob Cowper.

Lawry's side were back in complete control.

Bob Barber (20) and John Snow (18*) got England up to 165, allowing the home side to avoid the follow-on. However, they had lost 10/79.

Overall, the innings had lasted 104 overs. That, in anyone's language, is batting yourself into a hole. Even in the 1960s this particular English batting line-up should have made at least an extra 100 runs in the time they occupied the crease. Australia had only batted 130 overs for 357!

Australia had a first innings lead of 192 and were indebted to Doug Walters (86) for raising the advantage to 412. Pat Pocock, having recovered from his first innings mauling and with the wicket now giving his off-spin serious assistance, took 6/79.

The lead was plenty. England never looked like getting anywhere near the target. Colin Cowdrey suffered a double failure and Denis Amiss in his first Ashes Test completed a pair when bowled by Cowper.

The young Warwickshire batsman became "Wallaby" Cowper's sixth victim of the match. The triple centurion in the most recent Ashes Test would not have the impact he would have hoped with the bat on his second tour of England, but it was a huge bonus to Lawry in this game that he made such an impact with the ball.

For Amiss this was the first of his 11 Tests against Australia. Most were an unending torment. While he would average 46 with the bat overall in a 50-match career, it was a miserable 15 against Australia.

With the match lost on 5/105, England's batsmen finally offered some resistance. Barber and D'Oliveira added 80 before the former was caught in the gully on the final morning – Neil Hawke's only scalp for the match and his last ever in Test cricket. D'Oliveira kept going and was unbeaten on 87 when No.11 Pat Pocock was trapped in front of his stumps by Gleeson on the back foot to give Australia victory by 159 runs.

2nd Test

England had come back from their tour of the West Indies in early April 1968 cock-a-hoop having knocked the world champions from their perch with a 1-0 win in the five-match series.

They knew that Australia's recent record overseas was poor and that Lawry's side was the youngest Ashes squad ever, lacking many members with experience of English conditions.

They rubbed their hands with glee. The Ashes were as good as in the bag.

Then they were humiliated in the first Test. So, what do English selectors do when the people are angry? They swing the axe with the fervour of a Tudor executioner.

Onto the chopping block for their cricketing crime of compromising "team balance" went the two best performed

English batsmen in the first Test, Bob Barber and Basil D'Oliveira, along with Pat Pocock, despite his six-wicket second innings haul, Ken Higgs, and Dennis Amiss.

Higgs had been England's most consistent bowler in the previous two years but was never picked again. Thus his final Test bowling average of 20.74 is as good as the likes of Alan Davidson and West Indian greats Malcolm Marshall, Joel Garner and Curtly Ambrose. Not that even Higgs himself would believe he belonged in that company.

Barber's Test career was finished, too.

Into the side came Colin Milburn, much too large a man and aggressive batsman for the home-town batting to fall into another hole, Ken Barrington, one of the best performed Ashes batsmen of all time, Barry Knight, a bowling all-rounder rather than D'Oliveira whose cricket was balanced the other way, David Brown, a faster bowler than Higgs and from Colin Cowdrey's County of Kent, 23 year old left-arm medium paced spinner Derek Underwood for his first Ashes Test.

Australia was unchanged.

This was the 200th Test between Australia and England and was meant to be a celebration of the contests between the two countries. England had some fun at times. Generally, though, the game was yet another English damp misery.

The leading event on day one was a brutal hailstorm that stopped everyone in their tracks after England had reached 1/53.

Then on day two, after suffering some bruising on the fiery day-one wicket, burly No.3 Milburn played the innings of his life.

A tragic figure who lost an eye in a car accident the next summer and who died before the age of fifty, Milburn made the first hour and a half of day two his own by belting the ball to all parts with immense power and freedom.

His 83 at a distance of fifty years seems relatively insignificant. However, it showcased the huge talent of the overweight Geordie, sadly never to be totally fulfilled.

In contrast to Milburn, Essex all-rounder Barry Knight batted through the final 70 minutes of day two for 8 runs. The effect of that tardiness was magnified when day three was reduced to less than 14 overs and Cowdrey could not declare until the fourth morning.

Despite Milburn's superb batting and a typically solid contribution of 75 by England's Mr Ashes Ken Barrington, the wicket still offered the bowlers plenty. Australian wicketkeeper Barry Jarman found one delivery too hot to handle and broke a finger. Ken Barrington also took a whack on the finger from a lifter and one blow on the wrist kept Milburn out of the England side until the fifth Test.

With the sky overcast the Australian batsmen quickly got themselves into big trouble. Lawry was superbly caught down the leg-side by England's young wicketkeeping tyro Alan Knott.

Like Underwood and Cowdrey, he was from Kent and at 22 even twelve months younger than the left-armer with whom he would form a legendary partnership.

David Brown (5/42) was rampant and with England holding catches in the slips, the tourists slipped from 3/46 to 78 all out.

Brown completed Jarman's misery in the wicketkeeper's only Test at Lord's on three Ashes tours, by crunching his already damaged finger first ball.

But this match, similar in so many ways weather-wise and even score-wise (England made 77 in their first innings) to the equally damp Lord's Test of 1997, was doomed to fall short of a conclusion.

Back came the showers on day five. Australia saw their escape route and headed for it successfully, especially Paul Sheahan who batted the last 50 minutes of the match and then walked off on 0 not out.

3rd Test

Yet another Ashes Test totally wrecked by rain. The entire first day and almost all the last day were lost. Again the home side would lament the loss of time after they had assumed a very strong position. But the lack of actual cricket for the young tourists and damp English wickets was part of the reason they were able to dominate Lawry's team after Manchester.

England wanted their cake, and they expected to eat it too.

Birmingham does not quite have the bad weather reputation of Manchester, but it certainly knows how to rain properly there as well. In 2012, for example, the Test against the West Indies had three completely blank days.

In the time available in 2012 only 188 overs were bowled. In the three-and-a-bit days in 1968 the two sides got through 334 overs. That would be more than enough time to get a result in many Tests in 2025, especially in England. The Aussie disaster match at Nottingham in 2015 was completed in 175 overs.

The Edgbaston 2015 Test also finished in three days. In 1968 the four days attracted 56,000 patrons. The 2015 Ashes Test there saw 73,000 go through the turnstiles.

When England won the toss and batted at Edgbaston in 1968, the 409 they scored took them 172.5 overs. Even at less than three runs per over, it was felt the innings exhibited "English batsmanship at its finest."

There were moments of genuine significance. England captain Colin Cowdrey became the first man to play 100 Tests and he responded with a century. It was his 21st and second last Test 100. *Wisden* eulogised that Cowdrey played "beautifully," joining Wally Hammond as the only two batsmen to go past 7,000 runs in the entire history of Test cricket to that stage. There are some nice photos of Cowdrey's sumptuous drives in that innings, notably by the late Ken Kelly, in Cowdrey's book *The Incomparable Game* for example, but only a scrap or two of the filmed moment of him reaching his century seems to be generally available.

And the innings had its cost for Cowdrey and England. He never looked an athletic figure and the next summer he tore his Achilles tendon, missed virtually the entire 1969, had to handover the England captaincy and never got it back. At Edgbaston his glorious moment was sullied by a hamstring that ripped when he reached around 50.

He kept batting, admitting later that may have worsened the injury. He also had to endure the stress of having a reluctant, grumbling Geoff Boycott act as his runner for an extended period. Before being bowled for 104 on the third morning, Cowdrey had batted four hours and hit 15 fours.

Tom Graveney, another English batting classicist, who had his most productive series ever against Australia at the age of 41, got to 96 with 10 fours before being bowled by Australia's 1968 bowling hero Alan Connolly.

David Brown had already broken the finger of the Australian vice-captain at Lord's. Not satisfied with that, the Warwickshire fast bowler on his home turf put the tourists' captain, Lawry, out of this Test and the next one when he crushed his finger as well. By dismissing Lawry's opening partner Ian Redpath for a duck, Brown seemed to be establishing himself as Australia's main threat.

However, the emerging Ian Chappell (71) and Bob Cowper (57) were up for the fight and with Walters (46) backing them up at 5/213, the follow-on was avoided and the game on the fourth afternoon looked reasonably safe for the Australians.

Then the tourists' tail completely folded again. They found the accurate finger spin of Underwood and Illingworth almost unfathomable. England with a lead of 187 were back in with a chance of a victory. Edrich and Graveney added 74 in less than an hour, Graham McKenzie responded to possibly the briefest ever stint as Australian captain by bowling himself for 18 overs on the trot. Did he forget that he was in charge and that no one else would tell him to take his sweater?

England declared late on the fourth day with a lead of 330.

At 1/68 Australia's top order were making a fist of the last-day battle, but in the back of everyone's mind was the captain's injury and the "five out, all out" craw in the side of Lawry's team. Then it drizzled. Then it rained. Off the players went. It took three hours for the draw to be official; three hours of everyone sitting around and umpires' inspections and patrons drinking at the bar and calling out advice to the groundsmen and the umpires from the outer. At last play was abandoned.

4th Test

In the eyes of the English cricket world what this latest damp and frustrating Ashes series summer needed was a Dexter type of player. So, they went after him.

He was asked, very politely of course, whether he was available. He thought it was a splendid idea, even though he had hardly been playing.

So out he went and had a bit of a hit for Sussex against Kent at Hastings. And made a selection-clinching 203. He had reached his double century by hitting 6,4,6,4,3 off consecutive deliveries. It was within two runs of his highest ever score.

Dexter had arrived at the crease with Sussex 2/6 and suffered a bruised knee while batting. After his innings, therefore, he spent most of the game off the field.

Whatever his contribution on the field when he actually had to bat again in an Ashes Test, speculation about his return, then his actual coming out of retirement, gave the whole pre-match commentary and news profile a huge boost.

So, Dexter came in. Cowdrey (hamstring) and Boycott (back) went out with injury and Milburn (wrist) remained unavailable. Cowdrey was replaced as captain by Graveney. Then he too was in some doubt as he had a cut hand. It turned out that Graveney was available, but if he had failed a fitness test, who knows? Dexter might have been captain again!

England was in the midst of another of their selection merry-go-rounds, the type of which at times seems to be their speciality. Graveney would write that at Manchester at the nets prior to the first Test, "We went up there with enough players to man an army."

At Leeds for more justifiable reasons, there appeared to be a whole division of reinforcements, as well. Phil Sharpe, a local Yorkshire boy, was down near London at Southend-on-Sea when he was called up to the squad on the day before the match. His journey ended up a waste of time and petrol. England would select debutants Roger Prideaux and Keith Fletcher, as well as Dexter, ahead of him.

Australia had a debutant too; studious West Australian school teacher John Inverarity. Inverarity would have a stellar Sheffield Shield and teaching career and was respected as a coach and selector but would only play six Tests. Five of those six would be in England, his record modest.

After Jarman won the toss and batted the new man was soon bowled by a fired-up John Snow.

Inverarity, the direct replacement for Lawry, and certainly not a regular No.1 or No.2 had opened with Ian Redpath.

Redpath had made 97 on Test debut against South Africa back in 1963-64. This Leeds Test was the 20th appearance of the angular Victorian. Since his MCG start against South Africa his next Test best had been a battling 80 in a losing cause in Durban in January 1967 also against South Africa.

And despite some good scores against the Counties he walked out on the first morning at Headingley with only 95 runs in the series from six innings. The grumbles outside Victoria back in Australia were getting louder and louder that he was another to benefit from Jack Ryder's "pick a Vic first" supposed selection policy.

Snow, knowing England had to win to remain in the hunt to win the Ashes, bowled his fastest spell of the series.

"Snowy has not received the recognition he deserves over the years," Paul Sheahan said, "Maybe because he was not as charismatic as some of the other characters.

"But he was a great fast bowler. He had really strong shoulders and hit the deck hard. When you faced him he was always hitting the splice of the bat and in England he often got a remarkable amount of seam movement."

Snow beat the edge of Redpath's bat time and again. But when Redders struck the ball it flew off the middle with some force.

He hit 14 fours in three and a quarter hours, got to 92, had the hundred on toast then hit over an Illingworth delivery and was bowled.

It had been the most positive piece of Australian batting since Manchester. But it did not signal any special effort by the team to assert dominance. Redpath's partner in a second wicket stand of 94, Bob Cowper, at one stage played five successive maidens from the off-spin of Illingworth.

In all the left-hander faced 126 balls for his 27 including just one four. As the stockbroker was heading out the door of international cricket after this Test it was an unfortunate signing off.

With contributions from Ian Chappell (65), Doug Walters (42) and Paul Sheahan (38) before the traditional late order collapse (4/8), Australia made it to a competitive 315 in their first innings. As importantly for them and the Ashes they had consumed 133.4 overs of playing time.

It was enough to briefly give the tourists a significant advantage. With Alan Connolly (5/72) bowling his most rewarding Ashes spell, England slipped from 3/209 to 9/241.

Fletcher, the man from Essex who received preference over Sharpe, the man from Yorkshire who had driven all that way back to his home county from Essex and after missing a couple of slips catches, was caught behind down the leg-side for nought.

But in a 10th wicket rally, the type of which Lawry's side could only have dreamed about, No.11 Derek Underwood smacked 45 and put on 61 with No.10 David Brown.

In an hour Deadly Derek Underwood made more runs than Graham McKenzie and Alan Connolly did for Australia throughout 16 innings in the whole series!

Australia's first innings advantage was whittled down to 13. Caution became the priority.

The tactics were effective enough to consume another 147 overs while making 312. Fred Titmus may have been out of the line-up, however, off-spin could still dry up thoughts of shot-making among the Australians. Illingworth claimed 6/87. His combined second innings figures with fellow finger spinner Underwood were 96.1 overs 44 maidens 137 runs 8 wickets.

Redpath (48) completed a strong and personally successful match double while the contributions of the previously mentioned Chappell (81) and Walters (56) were crucial. Alan Knott claimed three stumpings off Illingworth.

Then came England's attempt to chase 330 to keep their Ashes hopes alive.

They did lose an early wicket, did score 230 from 84 overs and Australia did play defensively. But they were only four down by stumps. It is hard to imagine a current Test team not being prepared to be six or seven down before shutting up shop.

Again to refer to "Amazing Adelaide" in 2006 as a more modern example Australia chased 168 in 32.5 overs. But it was not a one-off. In 2013 England at the Oval made 5/206 in 40 overs chasing 227 before bad light ended the Test.

And in a very similar chase in 2001 at the same venue, led by Mark Butcher (173 not out), England chased 315 in 73.5 overs against an Australian side comparable with any in Ashes history. Admittedly, the Ashes were already decided in favour of Steve Waugh's champions on that occasion.

Back in 1968 the clearly rusty Dexter took 94 balls to make 38 and Fletcher hit one four in 70 balls. It was hardly a thrash.

Ken Barrington, THE English batsman of the 1960s, finished 46 not out. It was his final Test innings. In Australia during a single-wicket tournament that northern winter, aged 38, he suffered a heart attack and retired from all cricket.

Alan Connolly told Ken Piesse in 2010 how hard it was to penetrate Barrington's defences.

"When you bowled to Ken you never saw the stumps," Connolly said. "He had the widest bat and the widest set of pads. I didn't know I'd bowled him (Leeds Test 1st innings) until I heard a roar and here was this lovely snow-white Gray-Nicholls stump lying at Barry Jarman's feet."

In the first innings of his final Test the man from Surrey had batted three hours for 49. It was performance typical of much of his Test career. Despite the blazing innings in Melbourne in 1966 Barrington often batted in pedestrian fashion. He was dropped after making 137 against New Zealand in 1965 for slow scoring.

That approach, as effective as it was and it gave him 6,806

runs and a final Test average of 58, means that although a much-loved man, he is not listed amongst the absolute top echelon English players.

When *The Cricketer* magazine gathered a team of experts to vote for the greatest ever English batsmen, the list published in December 2017 had Barrington named 12th.

Not too shabby. It is, though, behind batsmen with clearly inferior numbers. E.W. Swanton for example rated Tom Graveney a superior batsman.

Is it Barrington's fault not many of his most significant innings led to victory? Or was it the fault of the bowlers, fieldsmen and defensive captains? Or was it just the misfortune of the era in which he played?

Tellingly, in the three Ashes Tests England won that Barrington played in, his scores were just 6 (Leeds '61), 35 and 0 not out (Melb '62-63) and 1 (Sydney '65-66).

Barrington's retirement was also the first breaking of the mould of players schooled in the 1950s who dominated the 1960s and saw nothing wrong with draw after draw in Test matches.

Ken Mackay, definitely schooled with the same batting attitude, wrote in 1966 that Barrington should produce three sons so that England would be unbeatable in the 1980s.

They may well have been unbeatable if that had transpired. They might not have won many games, either?

Funny, an everyone's-favourite-uncle type character, he did a fantastic job as England's Assistant Manager for several MCC winter tours. But he was full of nerves and stresses. Barrington, like his great adversary Wally Grout, could not shake his heart problems, and sadly died much too early of another heart attack at the age of just 50 while managing the England side in the West Indies early in 1981.

5th Test

This Test had many attributes the English love. Their team came from behind to level the series. They overcame the opposition and on the last day, the elements, to secure victory with just a few minutes to spare.

Joyously for the likes of television commentator Brian Johnston, and probably the disgust of the likes of Michael Parkinson, the victorious English XI contained just one player from a northern county.

Re-instated captain Colin Cowdrey had, including himself, three Kent players in this line-up. Yorkshire, despite winning their third consecutive County Championship in 1968 and their seventh title in 10 years, had one player in the side. But that one tyke, Ray Illingworth, would have his revenge on the south soon enough.

England did have the advantage of winning the toss in the best batting conditions of the series

They cashed in to the tune of making that 494. John Edrich who had churned out half centuries with ease all series converted the one he made on his home ground to 164. Basil D'Oliveira backed that up with his 158.

But it still took them 201 overs, almost two full days; Alan Connolly had to send down 57 of them.

Amidst all the bowling hard work by the Australians, Ashley Mallett dismissed Colin Cowdrey in his first over on debut. It failed to restore Lawry's faith in spinners as this was the day he and the young South Australian began their troubled on-field relationship.

The Australian outlook from the start of their first innings was that they could only seek a draw and continue to cling to their 1-0 lead. Compare that to England's successful effort to turn a match around when they chased South Africa's first innings score of 484 at the same venue in 2003. England thumped 604 in 162 overs and won the Test by 9 wickets.

The weather and pitch still impeccable at that stage, Australia's reply to England's 1st innings took the game into the fourth day and consumed 163.3 overs for 324 runs. That's less than two per over. Three per over, not unrealistic in modern times, would have given the Australians parity with England.

Lawry, in his element and trying to hold his team together, got to 135. He had a second wicket partnership with Ian Redpath of 129, but the non-Victorian Inverarity, Ian Chappell and Walters could only muster 16 between them.

It took the doggedness of debutant Mallett (43*) and fellow spinner Gleeson for the follow-on to be avoided.

England now had to get a rattle-on. Colin Milburn was back in the side and belted a six, the first by an Englishman in the series since the two he had hit at Lord's. In 2023 by comparison England hit 43 sixes in that Ashes series.

Soon though Milburn miscued a short ball to Lawry. England thrashed their way to 181 all out at the then-disrespectful rate of three runs per over. "The whole atmosphere was charged with electricity," wrote Bob Simpson in *The Australians In England 1968*.

They then removed Lawry and Redpath before stumps to have the tourists a shaky 2/13 by the close of the fourth day.

During the pre-lunch day five session, with Underwood causing difficulty as the pitch began to break up, Lawry's side were done and dusted at 5/65. Then, just on the interval, for the third Test of the five, a big thunderstorm arrived and rain fell in torrents.

The ground was literally under water and seemingly had saved Australia again. There are some great photos of the outfield covered with huge puddles and of Cowdrey scratching his head as he wades through the almost ankle-deep water.

Then a percentage of the spectators came onto the ground when the rain cleared. They mopped, spiked and helped push the water away in an attempt to get Kennington Oval fit for play.

Again, more than half a century later, it is a freedom of movement of fans to be wondered at.

On three counts 2025 is a different time.

Firstly, there were not many people in the ground on day five whereas attendance at The Oval for an Ashes Test now is so popular there is a ballot for ticket offers.

Secondly, for the several dozen hardy souls that were assisting on the outfield there would be huge fines, accumulating to hundreds of thousands of pounds between them for arena trespass.

And thirdly, a number of the volunteers were given very pointy sticks to make outfield drainage holes. In 1968 there was no improper use of them, but could it be guaranteed today that every one of those people would not use them on someone else as a weapon? "That could take yer eye out, that could."

Australians also wondered if the same spectators would have

been as motivated to dry the outfield if the situation of the game had been reversed.

After the result ABC radio commentator Alan McGilvray telephoned his friend former Australian captain Lindsay Hassett back in Melbourne from the London Cricketer's Club and complained, "They did us Lindsay, hundreds of people digging holes to get rid of the water – if England had been batting they would have poured pints of beer on the pitch."

The players got back on to the field at 4.45 pm and after some resistance by Jarman and Inverarity was broken by D'Oliveira, Underwood (7/50) ran through the Australian tail and England won at 5.55pm.

Brian Johnston was excited for Cowdrey again. "The happiest man on the field," Johnston called him.

Maybe so, but conversely John Inverarity was the saddest. He opened the batting, struggled through four hours for 56 and was within a few minutes of saving Australia from defeat when he was adjudged lbw not playing a shot at Underwood.

Oh, for a retrospective DRS to see if the ball would have hit the stumps.

"When he (Inverarity) was employed as Kent's Head Coach he jokingly used to try and avoid me whenever we found ourselves walking towards each other when I was at a Kent match. It was very funny," said Underwood.

Inverarity was the fourth Australian in the innings to be dismissed not playing a shot. It was taking defensive cricket to an extreme and was suitably penalised.

And so another Ashes series, the third of the last four, finished at that frustratingly inconclusive 1-1.

Fortunately, it is an Ashes series scoreline that has never appeared again.

But as previously mentioned, Barrington was gone. Dexter's comeback, although fun, was temporary and desperate from an England point of view, and had no real influence. Milburn for really those sad reasons, only played one more Test and 41-year-old Tom Graveney's Ashes days, despite his productive 1968, were over.

For Australia, Bob Cowper, who did not play at the Oval due to a broken thumb and who was not yet 28 years old, was finished as the Test cricketer. Stockbroking had become a more lucrative lure.

Neil Hawke, troubled by an old SANFL football shoulder injury and well known now as no fan of Lawry's leadership (and not yet 30 years old), apart from one match for Tasmania, never played any more first-class cricket.

Back in Australia in 1968-69 as Australia's men played the West Indies in a moderately-attended and divertingly entertaining series, Australia and England's women played a concurrent three-Test Ashes series.

Both sides had some great players. Enid Bakewell (England) and Miriam Knee (Australia) amongst them. But they had the same disease as the men. Three Tests; the series result? You guessed it; 0-0.

CHAPTER TEN

INTERLUDE NO.2; SAVE THOSE STEEL CANS, THEY COULD BE USEFUL

On January 22nd 1971 I attended an Ashes Test that I was fully committed to and old enough to appreciate. It had been a long time coming.

As previously mentioned, I had been to the MCG in February 1966 but that day was mostly lost in the mists of childhood immaturity and lack of sustained attentiveness.

Then there had been the barely an hour of Test cricket as the Indians subsided on January 3rd 1968 and a freezing anti-climactic and abbreviated Boxing Day at the other end of 1968 against the West Indies.

With Australia's Tests overseas for the entire summer of 1969-70, I had to be satisfied with regular attendance at some more Victorian games. Mostly they were Sheffield Shield matches, but Dad and I also went to one day of Victoria v New Zealand.

I clearly recall dashing out to the middle of the mighty Melbourne Cricket Ground arena when Victoria played Western Australia. My mission, to congratulate, with a pat on the back, the visiting prematurely grey-haired WA opening batsman, Terry Prindiville, upon him reaching what would be his only first-class hundred.

Armed with a sense of anticipation and a decent turn of speed, I was only the fourth fan in line of the dozens of invading boys to get my hand on the back of the opener's sweaty heavy flannel shirt. I was probably as proud as Prindiville.

These were good times, but the prospects of the next season, 1970-71, seemed even more enticing.

That was fine for me, however cricket was not getting any closer to moving outside the declining conservative mainstream. My Prindivile dash had been in front of less than 5,000 fans. Only twice in the entire season of 1969-70 had more than 10,000 people attended a first-class cricket match in Australia.

The Beatles might have recently and messily broken up, but even as solo artists, they and the blossoming pop/rock music industry were getting more radical and more culturally and politically influential.

There were so many revered albums released as the '60s segued into the '70s. Too many to mention them all here, but *Bridge Over Troubled Water* (Simon and Garfunkel), *Tapestry* (Carole King), *All Things Must Pass* (George Harrison), *After the Goldrush* (Neil Young) and *L.A. Woman* (The Doors) will do for a start.

This was the time of John and Yoko and the "Give Peace A Chance" movement. Students with long, long hair and, heaven forbid, beads and flowers and peace signs, marched and protested and sang songs.

Bill Lawry and Colin Cowdrey were rarely seen wearing beads. Nor were they asked their opinion on the Vietnam War.

I didn't mind. An Ashes series was coming to Australia and I couldn't wait.

My anticipation was fuelled further by the release of the *1970-71 ABC Cricket Book*. Like its 1968 predecessor, it is still sitting there in the top of my wardrobe. Just barely intact, its margins and scorebook pages are filled and scrawled with the numbers and results of the summer and the blotchiest most oversized attempts at marking a dot ball known to mankind. It was really hard to fit eight small circles and a number here and there into a space of approximately 5mm squared.

Then there was Eric Beecher's wonderful burgeoning magazine, *Australian Cricket*, with its tour previews and profiles. My Geelong-based hero Ian Redpath, one of the few to return from the 1970 tour of South Africa with an enhanced reputation, was the lead feature in the October edition.

I had also started cutting out and collecting newspaper photos of action in the Tests. There was a mere sprinkling from India and South Africa in 1969-70, but it was boom time in 1970-71.

There were whole centre spreads of Test cricket action of the Ashes series in *The Herald, The Sun* and *The Age*. My old school exercise book swelled with pride and newsprint and I would pore over the snapshots of the highlights of play with great delight. I kept these photo cuttings into adulthood, but they were moved into an outside shed and made a nice nest for an unpleasant rodent. Some gems were rescued; many were lost.

From late October the MCC 1970-71 tour of Australia built momentum in my mind. Three draws from four first-class starts did not discourage me as much as it did those cricket journalists wearied by almost a whole decade of '60s Ashes draws.

I had attended day two of the Vic v MCC match and watched in delight at home on television on ABC2 the locals cruise home by six wickets on day four. They were led to victory by none other than Geelong's own Redpath and Sheahan. Both hit two half centuries in the match.

So, the non-draw for Illingworth's side had been a loss. Then the first and second Tests also finished in draws. As had the next two first-class tour matches against the states.

In total the first ten first-class fixtures resulted in eight draws.

But that didn't matter to me because the Ashes Tests were coming to Melbourne. Between December 31 1970 and January 5 1971 Australia were playing England in the 3rd Test at the MCG.

I was going, maybe to all five days.

Or I was until Melbourne attracted a New Year rain depression.

Apart from the coin toss there was no cricket for three days. We drove to Melbourne from Geelong, sat in the MCG car park, watched rain hitting the windscreen, listened to the radio, but only briefly so as not to flatten the car battery, ate our sandwiches, walked around Swan St Richmond, then made the slow forlorn journey back home around the CBD, past the Docklands and through Footscray as we conceded defeat to Jupiter Pluvius.

My first Ashes Test proper was a washout. Never before and never since in Melbourne has a Test been abandoned to the weather.

The sun broke through on what would have been day four. What is now recognised as the first ever one-day international was scheduled instead of a two day Test. I went to the 40 eight-ball overs per side contest with a school chum and his family. Australia won. That was nice. I knew, however, deep down, it didn't matter. It wasn't a Test match.

I suffered TMDAG; Test match separation anxiety gloom. (I tell my wife I still do in winter). The Australian Cricket Board must have realised my plight. They dropped a Vic v MCC return match and a Vic Country v MCC match from the itinerary and added another Test.

This time it didn't rain. I couldn't get to day one but remember rushing up the many steps inside the MCG gate to see the first ball of day two from the standing room area in the old Southern Stand.

This, with setbacks, had been five years coming; longer in preparation than some big Hollywood movies.

There in front of me was my perfect panorama of green and white. The cricketers wore white towelling hats, baggy green caps and navy blue skull caps. I sighed in satisfaction, just the way I still can do today at a sun-drenched cricket landscape.

Ian Chappell, starting the day on 105 and Ian Redpath on 70, already had Australia at 1-260 as play resumed.

I anticipated great and sumptuous run-making from my heroes. But for that pair, at least, it was not to be. They were becalmed and then dismissed. Chappell, after one leg-glance boundary in the midst of a hook-or-don't-hook dilemma from an awkward defensive shot popped up a short ball to gully. Redpath after scoring just two runs in 45 minutes was bowled behind his legs.

Double breakthroughs by fast bowling pair John Snow and 21-year-old Bob Willis left the home side on 5/314.

I recall seeing Greg Chappell dismissed from the heavy shade of the Southern Stand. We then moved to the upstairs deck out of the strong January sun and witnessed the continuation of what looked a potentially fatal batting decline.

Australia did recover. Doug Walters danced around the crease in unconvincing fashion trying to counter short-pitched bowling by the England quicks. His waves and upper cuts still brought him a valuable 55. Then debutant Kerry O'Keeffe and "Iron Gloves" Rod Marsh combined to put Australia back on top.

Marsh, when set and after surviving a straight forward dropped catch in the leg-side outfield off Derek Underwood, thumped the ball about and reached 92 before Lawry controversially declared on 9/493.

He wanted a late evening wicket or two from his new-ball bowlers. But they were unthreatening and Lawry's declaration looked mean-spirited to Marsh, then without a Test hundred.

I had enjoyed probably the best day of the game. I returned each of the next three days as my first Ashes Test slowly and inexorably fizzled out to, not surprisingly, the inevitable, always at short odds, draw.

The end of the game was so dull that many of the 5th day attendees filled the last session with the monotonous beat of clanking empty drink cans on seats and the boundary fence. Their rhythm was far closer to a funeral dirge than the world's No.1 song at the time, 'My Sweet Lord' by George Harrison. They were noisily registering boredom and dismay at the meaningless batting of Boycott and Edrich. The police did nothing to quell the noise. They probably thought the protest was appropriate.

CHAPTER ELEVEN

DEMISE OF A CAPTAIN, BEGINNING OF AN ERA

"It was very difficult with Bill. I like Bill but he was very dour and never took any chances, but he would grab anything that you did."

Ray Illingworth was speaking about the 1972 Ashes series and comparing his Australian opposing captains on the old cricket VHS, *World of Cricket No.4* from 1993.

The 1972 series as will be shown later, was a great contest and a cricketing landmark turning point, but Illingworth's greatest personal achievement was to captain England to a 2-0 series win in Australia in 1970-71.

In 1968 the idea of the tough Yorkshire all-rounder leading his country in Australia would have seemed fanciful. But so astute was his leadership that by series end he had seen Lawry axed and he had joined an exclusive and elite small club of England captains who had captured the Ashes in Australia.

Not that everyone loved the way he went about it. The power of the southern counties that had been the dominant force in English cricket between 1956 and 1969 had been taken over by an uncompromising Yorkie.

His stamp was on the names that made up the MCC touring party of sixteen. Kent had won the 1970 County Championship and rightly had four players in the side. But unlike the previous tour all the extras in the team came from north of the Birmingham/ Leicester midlands line.

Mike Smith had Eric Russell as reserve opener, Peter Parfitt as back up batsman and John Murray as reserve wicketkeeper, all from Middlesex. David Allen (Gloucs), David Larter (Northants) and Barry Knight (Essex) fleshed out Smith's bowling attack.

Compare that to Illingworth's squad. John Hampshire, batsman, and Don Wilson, spinner, were Yorkshire ex-teammates of Illingworth. Neither made a big impact on the 1970-71 tour. His reserve wicketkeeper, Bob Taylor, was from Derbyshire and his fast bowling battery, although led by John Snow from Sussex, was at the start of the tour supplemented by Peter Lever (Lancs), Ken Shuttleworth (Lancs), and Alan Ward (Derby).

Michael (Barnsley Forever) Parkinson, approved. E.W. (Canterbury Rules the World) Swanton, did not.

A similar selection pattern emerged when Illingworth was appointed English cricket supremo in 1994.

Cowdrey, vice-captain in 1958-59, 1962-63 and 1965-66 seemed destined to have a turn in charge in 1970-71 until that Achilles tendon snapped during a Sunday League match for Kent in May 1969.

Illingworth, perhaps originally thought of as a stop-gap leader, was so successful in 1969 and in 1970 he rightly got the job. After leaving Yorkshire because of contractual disagreements, he had moved to Leicestershire.

In Cowdrey's absence, he led with panache, scored Test runs, claimed his share of wickets, cleaned up the West Indies and New Zealand 2-0 apiece, and despite the 1-4 scoreline, even pushed the star-studded Rest of the World side to the limits of their extensive talents.

Fit once more, Cowdrey returned to the side against the Rest of the World, but as vice-captain yet again. He was not pleased.

He and Illingworth later traded barbs in each other's various autobiographies.

Cowdrey's book *M.C.C.* is a great read and his comments are more guarded than Illingworth's.

Cowdrey had an ally in the 1970-71 tour manager David Clark, an ex-teammate at Kent. Illingworth might have had some influence in the selection of certain team members, however he had two people in leadership roles with whom he really didn't get along. This was in addition to coping with the other tough aspects of a tour of Australia. Apparently only level-headed physiotherapist Bernard Thomas, acting as mediator between factions, kept the rift between the team leadership group from turning into something really nasty.

Illingworth's clashes with leading Australian umpire Lou Rowan were another big problem for him during the 1970-71 Ashes series.

So, it was all stacked against the 38-year-old from Pudsey with the trademark wristy flick of the forelock across his thinning pate.

But he relished it.

A paid-up member of the everyone-else-is-at-fault-except-me club, Illingworth by any measure was as much to blame for the first two Tests of the 1970-71 series being unfinished as was Lawry.

Bill didn't give him much and he didn't give Bill much. In Brisbane it took within an hour or two of the end of day four for both first innings to be completed. These were eight-ball overs but re-calculated at six balls England's 464 was compiled at a rate of 2.37 runs per over.

In their two innings in Perth it was 2.23 and 2.13.

The highly criticised Melbourne Ashes Test of 2017-18 in Australia's incredibly slow match-saving second innings on a flat dull wicket, the run rate still was 2.11 per six-ball over.

Illingworth's on-field success prior to the tour didn't exactly get the heart racing or the turnstiles clicking with any greater speed than other recent tours either.

He had made no impact as an all-rounder on the 1962-63 tour of Australia. Behind Fred Titmus and David Allen then in the off-spinning pecking order, Illingworth played just two Tests, scored 57 runs in three innings and took one wicket for 131 runs.

Whatever the efforts of the ABC and Eric Beecher to lift cricket into the '70s many felt this was just going to be another Ashes drudgery filled stalemate.

A sixth Test was added in this series for the first time.

Perth was included in the Test itinerary, but not at the expense of an extra Melbourne or Sydney Test. So the sequence became Brisbane, Perth, Melbourne, Sydney, Adelaide, Sydney.

And then there was all that rain in the New Year in Melbourne.

What to do? A major money-spinner in a time when not much cricket money was being spun, was lost.

The Australian Board of Control and the MCC decided to stick in that other Test.

This meant for the one and only time in the entire history of not just Ashes cricket, but all Test cricket, not six, but seven Tests are recorded for the 1970-71 Ashes series.

That number seems incongruous in an era when authorities reckon two Tests is enough to constitute a series.

Between January 9th and February 17th 1971 four Ashes Tests

were played. If the seven Tests were never to be repeated a crowded program of continual back-to-back Tests was well ahead of its time and is now programmed as a matter of habit.

Unlike the modern players, Illingworth's side did still have rest days mid-Test. But the England captain and his team had no say in the final decision. They were not happy at the addition of the extra game in Melbourne, especially without the addition of an extra financial incentive.

"We nearly had a strike in Melbourne," John Snow said. "When we were told we were playing another Test and nobody said anything about money.

"I think Sir Don came into the room and said 'Thanks for agreeing to play the game lads.' That was the first we knew about it."

So confusing did the program end up that Ken Eastwood, one of the most intriguing one-Test-wonder stories of all time, thought the game he played in at the SCG, the seventh Test, was the extra one the authorities slotted in, not the Melbourne Test, now considered the fifth Test of the series.

In an interview for the Australian Cricket Society magazine, *Pavilion 2011*, Eastwood and I discussed his lengthy and exotic cricket career and his very brief but eventful Test appearance.

At the conclusion he said, "I always look back on my Test as such a bonus. After all if the Melbourne Boxing Day Test had not been washed out they wouldn't have added the 7th Test in Sydney and I would never have played Test cricket."

When I tried to point out that the Sydney Test he played in was always scheduled but that the earlier Melbourne Test had been added, Eastwood disagreed.

"I've been telling this story at Sportsmen's nights for years," he insisted. "The one I played in in Sydney was the one that was added on at the end of the summer. Not the Melbourne one."

I didn't continue with the argument but checked the fixture list in my *ABC Cricket Book* for the 1970-71 tour to prove to myself I hadn't been delusional.

I was right, but Eastwood's error was completely understandable.

The same mistake is repeated in the chapter on the 1970-71 series in Huw Turbervill's book *The Toughest Tour.*

The washout in Melbourne in January also had that other major effect. It brought about the sudden scheduling of the makeshift one-day game. This "exhibition" was meant to be a consolation for the thousands of Melburnians and their Victorian provincial and country cousins who had missed out on seeing any major international cricket over the New Year period.

The game provided instant entertainment for a healthy 40,000-plus crowd. The fans went home satisfied. The concept of the one-day international was born.

But before the seventh Test this, amongst a few individual landmarks, was the highpoint of the tour.

The on-going waning interest can be gauged from the fact that no tour book had been commissioned for publication.

In the third decade of the 21st century this may seem like Ashes trivia for only the most obsessive. It does need to be pointed out, however, that it was the first time this had happened since before the First World War.

In Dick Whitington's belated 1972 release, *Captain's Outrageous* his enthusiasm for the project, (was it written as a contractual obligation?) was hardly bursting out of the pages, especially as he titled the book *Captain's Outrageous.*

On page 14 he labelled the series, "The least attractive Test matches Australians have ever attended."

He sub-titled the book *Cricket in the Seventies* in attempt to separate it from the 1970-71 Ashes series. The front dust jacket photo is Doug Walters batting at Worcester in the opening match of the 1972 Ashes tour.

His titles for chapters three and four respectively are; "How Not to Win" and "How Not to Lose".

Like other books written by Whitington it is not a tour book in the purest sense anyway.

A product of a different time and class, Whitington was a good enough batsman to score Sheffield Shield centuries for South Australia. He was never seriously considered a Test candidate although he did apparently challenge one record for a cricketer: the number of marriages.

As a writer he is best remembered as the collaborator of a series of successful books co-authored with Keith Miller.

Mid-series, Miller in his newspaper column would also damn the series 1970-71 and the Ashes concept. After yet another drawn Test he wrote, "To hell with the Ashes. Dump them, get rid of them."

Apparently the Whitington-Miller series of books were the favourites of cricket loving, long standing Australian Prime Minister Sir Robert Menzies.

In each case Whitington addressed what he saw as the cricketing issues of the day before a second section of the books was devoted to a recently concluded tour and Tests. This was the format in 1950 and was unchanged in 1970 or 1972.

What was also locked into 1950 were his ultra conservative political views.

Whitington spent a lot of time in South Africa. In *Captain's Outrageous* he expressed his thoughts on how the outside world's view of apartheid was ignorant and how that view affected South African cricket.

Whitington provides overall Test attendance figures (608,486) and the gate takings ($483,317).

Although one extra Test, not including the Melbourne washout, was completed, these were a further decline on the numbers from 1965-66. The Saturday of the MCG Test in January 1971 saw 65,000 attend. The best gathering of the summer, it was 3,000 less than the highest in 1965-66.

Tours with two Tests in Melbourne, as had been the case in 1965-66, always had the ability to attract more spectators than when two Tests were played at the smaller-capacity SCG.

That should have been counterbalanced when in 1970-71 there was far less interference from rain than there had been five years previous.

By the conclusion of the 5th – sorry, 6th – Test, in Adelaide Australian captain Bill Lawry had made 324 runs against the English attack at an average of 40.5. He had completed three half centuries and was as cussedly determined at the crease as ever.

Again, outside the Ashes, there had been no problems getting results with Lawry at the helm. Australia defeated the West Indies in Australia in 1968-69. Lawry, Walters and Ian Chappell cashed in with big runs scored at a decent rate. The Adelaide Test, like the one eight years before had fast heavy scoring and finished in a thrilling nine-second-innings-wickets-down draw. Graham McKenzie, Alan Connolly and Johnny Gleeson claimed 76 wickets between them. The Frank Worrell Trophy, a much bigger and shinier piece of merchandise than the Ashes, was regained.

Then, India were overcome in India 3-1. The success in India in late 1969, battling illness, sub-standard transport and accommodation and riots, remains Australia's greatest ever in that country.

But Lawry's side then immediately after, in early 1970, lost 0-4 in South Africa and was 0-1 down in this Ashes series. Except for one session in Perth the home side had never looked to be in a position to push for a win. Lawry's 34th birthday was the day before the 7th Test.

Sir Donald Bradman and his fellow selectors then replaced Lawry as captain with Ian Chappell for the 7th Test. They also omitted Lawry from the team altogether for debutant Eastwood. The crew-cut Footscray stalwart was even older than his state teammate.

Lawry took the exceptionally heavy blow on the chin brilliantly. He continued to play for Victoria in the hope of being selected for the 1972 Ashes tour.

When he missed a spot there, being left out for clearly inferior players, he called time on his first-class career. Even then he continued playing club cricket in Melbourne for another summer or two.

While the selectors could make a strong enough, if clearly controversial case, for their decision their man-management of the Lawry sacking was archaic and ignorant.

Lawry had been a dedicated leader of his country's cricket team for four seasons and 26 Tests. To most cricket followers the decision was a large shock. No Australian Test captain had been sacked for more than 40 years or longer, depending on how you view the dismissal of Jack Ryder in 1930.

But no selector contacted Lawry. He found out from teammates Keith Stackpole and Ian Redpath who had just moments before been informed by Adelaide journalist Alan Shiell.

Replacing Lawry with Ian Chappell was the point at which Gideon Haigh felt it was appropriate to conclude his fine book about cricket in Australia between 1946 and 1971, *The Summer Game*.

He points out that clearly Chappell, six years younger, was the child of a different generation to Lawry.

"Ian Chappell and I are great friends, but we are chalk and cheese," Lawry admitted.

True, but in addition Chappell was more belligerent in his attitude to the cricketing authorities. He was also more conscious of his appearance, not averse to wearing ties with floral patterns or not wearing a tie at all.

More in the style of Richie Benaud, he aligned himself with the Keith Millers of the cricketing world. His father told him to watch Miller when the young Chappell was taken to matches at the Adelaide Oval in the 1950s. His legendary Test captain and grandfather Vic Richardson, another obvious influence, told him to never captain a side like a Victorian.

The brand of bat he used was obvious. Ian and Greg Chappell's Gray-Nicholls with a sword stripe down the back was a brilliant early piece of sponsorship and television marketing.

Ian's shirt was always open to the about the third or fourth button. He fielded in a white towelling hat.

Lawry never took off his baggy green. He cited the likes of Jack Ryder, Len Maddocks, Neil Harvey and Colin McDonald as influences.

Chappell would risk losing a cricket match to get a win, even an Ashes Test.

Lawry had been the second iconic cricketer of the 1960s to be dropped from the team in the middle of the series.

Leading fast bowler Graham McKenzie was demoted after the loss in Sydney in the 4th Test.

After bowling well in India Garth McKenzie could barely raise a gallop in South Africa and finished that four-match series with just one wicket for 333 runs.

Back in Australia after a season with Leicestershire in County Cricket in 1970 he had by the completion of the 4th Test against England just seven wickets at 50.14. That included match figures of 1/139 in the Sydney loss.

McKenzie would later admit his stamina was not what it should have been at that time. So, like Lawry, he did not complain about his omission.

Also like Lawry, he did not end his career. McKenzie played County Cricket again in England in 1971 and turned out for Western Australia in 1971-72.

He was then selected for the first two internationals against the Rest of the World that summer and had a fine spell in the second innings in Perth where he claimed four wickets.

Then he was told he would be rested so that other 1972 Ashes tour contenders such as Bob Massie could be assessed.

To McKenzie that seemed fair enough, except that when the team of 17 for the 1972 Tour of England was announced big Garth's name was not there.

Like Lawry, he was not told why he was no longer in favour. And like Lawry his Test career was over. Indeed it symbolically finished with a smack in the face from a sharply lifting John Snow delivery on the fifth day of the 4th Test, January 14th 1971. McKenzie's Test wicket tally was 246, just a tantalising two short of Richie Benaud's then Australian record 248.

At the time that seemed significant and the actions of the selectors cruel. Now, as Shane Warne holds top spot with 708 it seems less so, from a statistical point of view at least.

But equally so, the bevy of fast bowlers who followed McKenzie – Alan Thomson, Ross Duncan, Tony Dell, Jeff Hammond, David Colley and even Bob Massie – were clearly short of Test class either in ability or durability, or both. Dennis Lillee was the exception.

To drag in a modern comparison again, the selectorial treatment of McKenzie at the age of 30 compares very unfavourably with someone more recently such as Peter Siddle.

Siddle, probably a notch down on the talent of McKenzie, was kept in the Australian Test squad until he was 35, his skill, knowledge and experience being put to effective use into his mid-thirties.

In the late '50s post-war fast bowling legend Ray Lindwall was recalled to Richie Benaud's side when aged in his late 30s. Like Siddle, he also played a valuable role for a year or two.

There is no doubt McKenzie could so easily have done a similar job for Ian Chappell's side in the early '70s.

CHAPTER TWELVE

1970-71 THE TESTS

While patrons through the gate at Ashes Tests continued to decline in 1970-71 the number of people who actually watched the action in Australia probably broke all sorts of records by huge margins.

Coverage of Ashes Tests in England by the BBC had been reasonably extensive in the 1960s. Much of it ball by ball. However, it had to be flipped between BBC1 and BBC2 and there were all sorts of interruptions to the coverage for kids' programs, news reports, horse racing, rowing, equestrian and other varied sporting and non-sporting events.

In Australia in 1970-71 the ABC committed itself to almost exhaustive coverage of the entire series. Only the post-tea session would be televised in the city hosting the Test, but the whole day's play was covered from interstate cities.

It was groundbreaking and is now standard practice around the world. The ABC's coverage was superb for the era and the budget available.

Problems did occur, though. The momentous groundbreaking Gabba Test died as a spectacle after a promising start and getting pictures across from Perth to the east coast was technologically very difficult in late 1970.

On the Saturday the link broke down somewhere out there in the desert near the Great Australian Bight, so it was back to the radio for cricket coverage.

Sunday, day three, the pictures had been restored and almost all of Australia had the opportunity to see the wonderful debut Test innings by Greg Chappell.

The drama grew during the afternoon as Chappell and Redpath re-built the Australian innings from a precarious position.

The young South Australian reached 98. Australia waited with bated breath. Then, to the absolute astonishment and disappointment of hundreds of thousands, perhaps millions of viewers on the east coast, it was time to leave the cricket for the broadcast of the 7.00pm news.

Where was Kerry Packer when you needed him? No one at the ABC ever took full public responsibility. Probably at the next meeting the executives admitted they had all learned a very valuable lesson.

At the same meeting they had perhaps also discussed that companies at one venue were gaining free advertising on the national broadcaster and that was against their constitution.

At the Gabba the fences were covered in advertising hoardings. To my knowledge this was the first time fence space had been sold for advertising in Test cricket.

Tobacco companies featured prominently in the premium behind-the-wicket positions.

The domestic one-day competition may have had a banner or two hanging on the fence announcing the sponsor of the matches. At the Gabba they took the idea much further, however.

Like back-to-back Tests and exhaustive coverage of matches, fence space being sold for advertising is now standard practice at all sporting events, not just cricket.

The Queensland authorities who thought of the idea could pat themselves on the back.

Nor were they finished with their think-outside-the-square ideas. When England returned for the next Ashes Test at the Gabba in 1974 a greyhound track had been added to ring the outfield.

This remained an unusual feature of the Gabba for the next 20 years.

It was eventually removed and, unlike fence advertising hoardings, never caught on at other venues.

Chappell reached his 100 at the WACA and footage of that entire session plus the Gabba and two Sydney Tests was played on ABC's *Late Night Legends* when that was aired several years ago.

I have copies and enjoy them from a nostalgia perspective. Some of it is hard work, though, and the sense in Brisbane that the game will not reach a conclusion is palpable and deflating throughout the final two days.

The 7th Test was far more dramatic. Like 1968, the players saved their best till last. If the early stuff had been a laborious at times, the climax where England bowled out Australia to regain the Ashes was gripping.

Footage of the Australian second innings that ends with Illingworth being chaired off the SCG by grateful teammates crops up on many Ashes DVD and VHS compilations in all its black and white glory.

The increase of colour photographs of the matches lifted the apparent attractiveness of the product. A number of shots, particularly of the seventh Test, were published in books with Jack Pollard's trademark.

Australian Cricket magazine also had fine moments captured on several covers. The shots of John Snow in his bowling follow-through in the early tour match in Adelaide and Alan Thomson bouncing Brian Luckhurst in the Melbourne Test are iconic colour images of the era.

More were to be found in the *Australian Cricket Yearbook* 1971. There, though, they were buttressed by articles titled, 'Test Cricket... Where To Now?' and 'The Pros. – And Dullsville?" written by E.W. Swanton and Frank Tyson respectively.

Clearly, despite media technological advances, the Ashes still had a major image problem at the start of the 1970s.

At least it had a significant result. England's 2-0 series win gave them a rare away Ashes success and regained the Urn for the tourists after 12 years.

And there could be no question as to the superior team over the entirety of the summer. England's attack was relatively stable with several consistent contributors and a fast-bowling spearhead, while Australia struggled for wickets and made changes to its bowling line-up every game.

Arguably John Snow was the difference. The Sussex speedster took virtually double the number of wickets of any other bowler on either side.

Australia's new fast bowling secret weapon, Alan Thomson, was supposed to intimidate the Englishmen in the way his namesake would do with much more brutal effect four years later. He had been impressive for Victoria in 1969-70 and at the start of 1970-71.

However, his skippy-flippy windmill action was physically unsustainable. He rarely troubled the top-line English batsmen who saw his bouncers coming and had little trouble eluding them. He could bowl a huge in-swinger with the new ball, but it began to move as soon as it left the hand. He was no-balled many times and may have been lucky to escape further calls because his back foot often looked to have cut the return crease at the point of delivery.

Thomson feels he was unfortunate and was forced out of his comfort zone somewhat.

“Dropped catches fixed me up,” Thomson said. “I was told I had to get a wicket or knock someone’s head off. They wanted me to hit them in the head and bounce even Snowy. I had common sense. I’m not brave. I’m not suicidal.

“In Adelaide he started to pitch them short to me, very short. He was fast alright.”

Snow could lift the ball into the batsmen’s throat area from just short of a length.

He temporarily messed up Ian Chappell’s mind about whether to hook or not, caused Doug Walters to back off and slash on the off-side aka Bradman in the Bodyline series, clunked the heads of Graham McKenzie and Terry Jenner on the sporting surfaces prepared in Sydney and totally demolished the Australian second innings in the 4th Test with 7/40.

The son of a vicar, Snow strutted and pouted around Australian outfields in a moody fashion that would have made Mick Jagger proud and he irritated the Australian fans to such an extent they rioted after Jenner was hit in the 7th Test.

There was media tut-tutting, but Snow was another sign that, despite the on-going problems, maybe there was light at the end of the Ashes entertainment tunnel.

Most importantly, aged just a few months younger than McKenzie, Snow was at his peak as a mature, accurate and effective fast bowler.

What surprised Australians was that they did not see Snow coming. Any rational assessment based on previous records seemed to suggest he would be no more of a threat than Jeff Jones and David Brown had been in 1965-66.

However, he joins Tyson and Larwood before him as fast bowlers who led the way for England to win an Ashes series Down Under.

Despite some brave and aggressive efforts by the likes of Bob Willis in 1978-79, Graham Dilley in 1986-87 and Jimmy Anderson in 2010-11, Snow is really the last English fast bowler to seriously disturb the equilibrium of Australian batsmen in their own country over a whole series and make them think about their physical wellbeing.

1st Test

One annoying factor in all these drawn Tests is the number of times a team would assert their dominance with aggressive cricket at one point in the match, then back off and slow down to consolidate their position.

Both Australia and England were guilty of this at the Gabba.

After Lawry won the toss the home side dominated day one on the back of a breakthrough innings by his fellow opener and Victorian teammate, Keith Stackpole.

Stacky made 175 of his eventual 207 as the series was launched, out of his team's 2-308. He was especially severe on Derek

Underwood who had held such a stranglehold on the Aussie batsmen in 1968.

A genuine thumper of the ball, Stackpole kept lofting the left-arm medium paced finger-spinner into the unofficial cow-corner of the Gabba.

Yet, as impressive as this was, Stackpole did not score a run against the fatigued Englishmen in the final 30 minutes of the day.

On day two it seemed even more consolidation was required. Australia added only 76 runs to be 3/384 at lunch. The objective of the home side was to bat England out of the match with a total near 500.

Then from nowhere Underwood ripped the heart out of the Australian middle order. This galvanised John Snow who, gaining a little of what was then undiagnosed reverse swing, demolished the inexperienced and fragile tail and from 4/418 Lawry's side lost 7/15 to be all for 433.

It looked like 1968 all over again.

If Australia's innings was a thing of two distinctly different halves, England's was one continuous steady drone. Almost from ball one they looked like they would make something between 463 and 465. Of the first seven batsmen, John Edrich top-scored with 79 and Colin Cowdrey had the lowest total with 28.

The disgruntled former captain did become the then highest Test run-scorer of all time on day three when he passed Wally Hammond's aggregate of 7,249 runs. It seemed a big achievement then, but since the top total in 2025 is Sachin Tendulkar's 15,921 the significance has shrunk a little.

On the fourth day the game almost ground to a complete halt.

An hour was lost to rain. England, although they could not really lose from a position of being 68 behind Australia with four wickets standing, batted on until the tea break for their precious lead of 31.

Australia's attack lacked any venom. Part-timer Doug Walters finished with the incongruous figures of 3/12. It meant in his two most recent home Ashes Tests his little swingers had claimed 7/65.

Walters' bowling successes came from just 5.5 overs (45 deliveries). That contrasted strongly with fast bowling debutant Alan "Froggy" Thomson. The man with what must be the most unorthodox bowling action in Test cricket pre-Paul "frog in a blender" Adams of South Africa, sent down 296 deliveries for the match while claiming 1/156.

Australia responded in kind in their second innings with a brick wall mostly built by their captain.

Lawry's feature shot was the guided glide to third man. When the ABC showed the fourth day's highlights package it featured dot balls and the captain changing the field. There were not enough boundaries and wickets to fill the time allotment.

The fifth day was no better. Lawry ensured the draw with his five and a half hour 84, breaking his team's losing sequence of four. Eventually he became one of part-time leg-spinner Keith Fletcher's two scalps in 59 Tests.

Australia batted at a rate of 1.71 runs per six-ball over in their second innings. Keith Stackpole who had made 175 on the opening day batted 82 minutes for eight in the second dig.

With most of the 2,396 in attendance by now generally looking the other way, the Australian tail still managed to lose their last four wickets for 21 as the game reached its death throes.

However, they would have seen one of cricket's greatest ever quirks of fate if they watched the very last ball of the match. Geoff Boycott just had to defend a Terry Jenner delivery to get another personally precious not out. Instead, he drove a catch straight back at the leg-spinner. To be dismissed in such a way would have haunted the single-minded Yorkshireman for a very long time. Especially as eventually it cost him a Test series average of 100.

Even patient and respectful much-loved Australian journalist Ray Robinson finally joined the chorus of condemnation.

In the January 1971 edition of *Australian Cricket* he wrote; "In a way it is just as well there are six Tests in England's present series in Australia.

"You may ask in what way? Surely one Test like Brisbane's was enough without extending such boredom to an extra city! What I mean is a six Test series gives greater opportunity to live down the bad impression left by an interest-killing start that dismayed cricket fans all over the country.

"Instead of crowds thronging to see an exciting climax to an international contest fewer than 2,400 thought the last day of the Brisbane Test worth watching.

"How did the degeneration gap between pre-season pledges and field tactics open up? Where did the unfortunate men who found the occasion too big for them go wrong?

"Can either captain put his hand on his heart and deny that he was more concerned with the slightest possibility of becoming one down than with any other result in the first Test? That is how it looked to every ex-international I've heard express an opinion. In seven years since Richie Benaud gave up the Australian captaincy we seem to have lost sight of what he put first- the over-riding importance of seizing and holding the initiative."

The writer of two of the best ever Australian cricket books, *Between Wickets* and *On Top Down Under,* Robinson emphasised his point with a broadcasting box anecdote.

"Next to the patience of customers who wouldn't come back again, nothing was worn thinner by the brakes-on Brisbane Test than broadcasters' vocal chords," he wrote.

"When runs were rarer than rhinestones, radiomen are not free to read newspapers, doze off, withdraw to the bar or go home.

"Dividing each hour into thirds, the ABC rosters each soundman for 20-minute turns describing the match (I nearly said the play). When this becomes indescribable without resorting to bad language, broadcasters trying to keep listeners interested are under more tension than the most upright batsman.

"On a day when 31 runs an hour crept on to the board Alan McGilvray had just completed a 20-minute stretch when Lindsay Hassett began his end-of-over comments by saying: 'Congratulations, Alan, I think you got four runs in that session'."

2nd Test

The WACA began its life as an Ashes Test venue, indeed as a Test venue, on December 11th 1970.

It finished that reign, as an Ashes ground at least, 47 years and one week later. England would win once in Perth in 14 attempts. And that was against an Australian side decimated by World Series Cricket defections in 1978-79.

There would only be three Ashes draws there. The first ever

WACA Test was, of course, one of them.

It took only three days for the Gabba Test to die as a spectacle. At least the WACA's debut Test threw up the possibility of a result until lunch on the final day. After that everyone again knew what its destiny would be.

Australia, no doubt sick of five all-out situations, strengthened its batting depth by debuting Greg Chappell at No.7.

That allowed them to get out of a hole in their first innings, but when they had a sniff of victory in the second innings, it meant that their attack was too thin to push on to success on the final day.

The home side, as they had with Stackpole in Brisbane, once more provided the individual batting highlights.

Like his fellow Victorian at the Gabba, Ian Redpath compiled what would remain his highest ever Test score. Redders made 171, his second Test ton.

He would be overshadowed though by the younger Chappell brother, Greg, who scored 108 on debut.

The 22-year-old walked to the wicket with Australia on 5/107 chasing England's first innings of 397. Chappell, showed concentration, technique and determination. He had made just 12 after an hour and a quarter and took more than three hours to reach his maiden Test fifty. "Not terribly fluent," admitted ABC TV commentator Frank Tyson.

Then, with a series of elegant on-drives, he took less than an hour to turn his half-century into a glorious hundred.

His 219-run sixth-wicket partnership with Redpath, particularly after tea on day three, was the Australian batting highpoint of the summer.

While his impact on the rest of the series would be more modest, it was clear Australia had unearthed a talent of significance. Greg Chappell would mould a career that saw him still held in equal argument beside Ricky Ponting and Steve Smith as Australia's best ever since Bradman.

Australia took a first innings lead of 43 and following a double breakthrough by Gleeson and a bonus wicket from Thomson, reduced England from 1/98 to 4/101 late on day four.

Lawry's limited attack was unable to press on to victory, though. John Edrich, a Surrey disciple of Barrington, set up camp for nearly six hours and guided England out of trouble with 115 not out.

It was the second English century in the match. Opener Brian Luckhurst had made 131 on day one to become the first Test centurion at the WACA. England openers Luckhurst and Boycott, once more finding little menace in the new-ball fast bowling of Graham McKenzie and Alan Thomson, had opening partnerships of 171 and 60.

For Australia, though, John Snow was becoming a bigger and bigger handful. The home side had been 3/17 in the first innings and was 3/40 on the last day before that great batting survivor and captain, Lawry, held out the threat for two and a half hours. He walked off at stumps on day five with Redpath, unbeaten on 38. Lawry could argue it was a necessary rear-guard action. It had condemned the WACA's first historic Ashes Test to the same fate as most of the rest, however.

Lawry's day five graft was almost a reprise of his innings in the 5th Test in 1962-63. The target, situation and final score were very similar. So was the opinion of E.M. Wellings. This time the acerbic writer found voice as *Wisden*'s correspondent in Australia.

"Lawry was craven," Wellings wrote. "His second run completed his 5,000 in Test cricket, his third his 2,000 against England. With that he seemed content. After sixty-eight minutes he had made only 6."

The five Victorians in the Australian side, including Lawry, were given such a hard time by the West Australian fans at times during the Test that they thought they were playing for the away team.

Vultures were gathering.

3rd Test

The 3rd Test consisted of an exchange of team sheets, a coin toss, a decision by Illingworth to send Australia in and lots and lots of rain.

The most memorable single moment of that week was the photos of Sir Donald Bradman in his pyjamas and dressing gown addressing the media while holding a cup of tea and a piece of toast. He announced the abandonment of the Test and the playing of the 40 eight-ball overs per side one-dayer.

It was lauded as a progressive positive move across the Anglo-Australian cricketing media.

4th Test

Australia won the one-dayer convincingly by six wickets. The SCG Test, though, starting just four days later proved as white-ball cricket often does, that ODI or T20 success means very little as an indicator of who might win a follow-up five-day game.

After two days of a tight, fluctuating contest on a dry wicket, Ray Illingworth's tourists smashed the home side by 299 runs. The win only gave England a similar series margin to the one they could not hold on to in the previous two Ashes series Down Under. This time, however, it looked like they had exposed a real gap in the quality of the two teams.

The miserable match payments to players by the Board of Control were beginning to bite to the detriment of Australia. Bob Cowper had retired at the age of 29, Bob Simpson quit Test cricket still in his prime aged 32, and Australia's two best performed fast bowlers of the late 1960s, Alan Connolly and Graham McKenzie, had signed contracts with County sides Middlesex and Leicestershire to boost their modest international incomes.

Aged 31 and 29 respectively, they shared the new-ball in this Test and over the whole match claimed one wicket apiece. They both lacked stamina and any sustained pace and penetration. Boycott made 77 and 142 not out and cruised through the two innings.

On day one the cover-driving of the Yorkshireman was Dexteresque in its power and ability to take the attack to the bowling. It is hard to know if that is an accolade Boycott would even enjoy.

But Dexter himself wrote that Boycott's second innings century, his first in Tests against Australia, was the best innings he had ever seen on a bad wicket.

This is also probably the innings where D'Oliveira walked up to Boycott in the midst of their fourth wicket partnership of 133, which shut Australia out of the game, and said he had deciphered the wiles of John Gleeson's mystery spin. Boycott allegedly said he had done exactly that ages ago, but that they shouldn't let any of those "other bastards" (in the dressing room) know.

So disappointed was Connolly by his form and follow-up omission, he retired almost immediately after this SCG game. McKenzie, too, fatigued and suffering from low blood pressure, took a break from all cricket for the remainder of the summer, except a few limited-over matches.

Richie Benaud introducing the BBC highlights package after day two had a real glint in his eye. Usually phlegmatic and calm, the voice of the former captain and leg-spinner sounded excited in proclaiming that this match was heading for a result. Yes folks, a result!

Benaud's enthusiasm did not translate into extra people coming through the turnstiles. Despite its premium New Year calendar slot, this SCG Test pulled in just 101,694 fans over five days. That number compared very unfavourably with the 1962-63 equivalent Test attendance of 166,626 and the 130,759 in 1965-66.

It was even marginally less than the number who went to the 1968-69 Test against the West Indies.

By comparison, in 2013-14 and 2017-18 the numbers for the first three days of the SCG New Year Ashes Test were back up to over 40,000 per day. Covid affected attendances at the 2021-22 SCG Ashes Test. But it was still higher over the whole match than in 1970-71.

Chasing 332, Australia was 4-189 at stumps on day two. Redpath and Stackpole, not out overnight, were photographed by the *Melbourne Herald* in the swimming pool on the rest day at the team hotel and lauded them as Australia's two hopes to gain a worthwhile first innings lead.

Resuming on day three, Redpath was caught at slip from the first ball of the opening over and Stackpole was dismissed soon after. "Oh Ian! Oh Keith!" lamented the same newspaper that evening.

Redpath had at least contributed 64 and had put on 97 with Walters. Lawry struggled for 85 minutes to make nine. He batted like a man who could not find a way to make a run. Although he could take some shine off the new-ball Lawry was unable to give any batting impetus to his side.

Later in the game as Australia collapsed disastrously to John Snow, Lawry showed courage and resolve and carried his bat for 60 out of 116. Once more, however, this was an attempt to save Australia rather than put them in a winning position. As noble as was his application, defensive technique and concentration, it was never going to change the result.

To make matters even worse for Lawry, his effort to revive his team's fortunes by re-jigging the batting order failed miserably.

Back in 1968-69, also at the SCG, Lawry had boosted the flagging contributions of Keith Stackpole and Ian Redpath against the West Indies by swapping their places in the batting order. Lawry took Stackpole out to open and dropped Redpath down to No.5. Then it worked for all concerned. Stackpole made 58 and Redpath 80.

This time it was Stackpole, struggling badly after his double century in Brisbane, who was protected from the new-ball. Ian Chappell, usually first drop, walked out to open the batting with his captain.

Stackpole at No.6 scored just enough runs to keep his place. Chappell though, made 12 and, failing to cope with a lifting John

Snow delivery, a second innings first-ball duck. Much to his relief he would immediately return to No.3, never having to open a Test innings again.

He always insisted, even if he had to face the second ball of the innings, the batting psychology at No.3 was significantly different to being No.1 or No.2. For him, at least.

On the last day, Graham McKenzie suffered a facial injury from John Snow's bowling that caused him to retire hurt with a bleeding nose.

It surprised me to read in that December 2017 edition of *The Cricketer*, that writer James Coyne got this incident very muddled with the later blow to the head of Terry Jenner in the 7th Test.

The hit on McKenzie although unpopular, unpleasant and unfortunate failed to start a bottle-throwing riot. It is quite hard to summon a riot out of a crowd of 4,241 spread right around a cricket ground. They wouldn't have had that many bottles between them in the middle of a first session anyway.

Coyne wrote that Jenner was hit in the face and quoted Snow's figures for this Test. Jenner though, would later be hit in the back of the head in the 7th Test and Snow, finding the long tour was taking a physical toll, claimed 1/68 in that innings.

See, again, having seven Tests confuses everyone.

5th Test

Annoyed at not being consulted about the changes to their itinerary, Illingworth's England spent a lot of this historic re-scheduled Melbourne Test trying to keep their one-nil series lead intact.

Against Australia's eager but ultimately ineffective bowling attack, achieving another draw was not difficult.

The Test began with a wave of publicity about it being a sign that Australian cricket's administrators were moving with the times at last and ended with the bored fifth day crowd of 10,000 banging those empty beer and soft drink cans on the metal pickets and the railing of the MCG fence. They were protesting the tedium and pointlessness of what was on the cricket field in front of them.

Like Brisbane, the Test began with a bit of Aussie batting spark and finished with them going through the bowling motions, failing to take an English second innings wicket.

There was one significant event, or significant innings, at least, that had great impact on the future of Australian cricket, but is largely overlooked now.

Australia's vice-captain, Ian Chappell, came into this Test under a fair bit of pressure to hold his place in the side.

Chappell played this innings "with his Test career in the balance," wrote Eric Beecher in the March 1971 edition of *Australian Cricket* magazine.

After a disastrous tour of South Africa where he made just 92 runs at 11.5, Chappell had failed to make much impact on the 1970-71 Ashes series. Following the failed experiment of opening the batting in Sydney, Chappell's 1970-71 figures, were 59, 10, 50, 17, 12, and 0. That's an unimposing 148 runs at an average of less than 25 in the three Tests played. Another bad match in Melbourne must have brought up his name before the selectors as to whether he was due for a rest.

What if he had failed and was dropped? What would have

happened to Australian cricket over the next couple of years? In another parallel universe, where Ian Chappell was omitted and faded into the background, whole long chapters of the history of Australian cricket would be written differently.

Restored to his favoured No.3 batting spot, Chappell arrived at the crease on day one and he did for a time scratch around like a man whose bat had no middle. He offered chances to slips off Snow and D'Oliveira. Colin Cowdrey, whose recall to the England side after being left out in Sydney could not have gone worse, grassed one straightforward offering at slip off Basil D'Oliveira. It was one of four he would put down in a personally disastrous match.

There was some early juice in the wicket. D'Oliveira, only medium pace but accurate, was a handful. Getting the ball to seam around and bounce with venom, he whacked Bill Lawry on the ends of the fingers and caused him to temporarily retire hurt.

With fortune, Chappell survived that tough period and the huge crowd invasion when he reached his 100. The rush onto the ground of kids and inebriated young adults bent on souvenir procurement of players' caps and bails was in such large numbers and so disruptive it saw the habit immediately banned that very evening. In some parts of the world it took longer than others, but it is illegal to enter the playing arena during play everywhere now.

In New Zealand they do still allow parading and scratch-match cricket on the outfield during intervals at some venues. And a treat it is.

As the sun dried the pitch and the seam flattened on the ball, D'Oliveira's threat waned on day one. Suddenly Chappell's pull and cut shots were working again to the tune of a dozen boundaries. In the post-tea session he added 125 runs with the consistent Redpath. Chappell batted as confidently as he had against the West Indies on the same ground two years previously when he was in a rich vein of form and made 165. In the short term his position in the side was no longer in doubt and never would be again. Ultimately his place in the history of the game in Australia would be assured.

Australia, on the back of Chappell's 111 and Rod Marsh's first significant Test innings of 92 not out, made 9/493dec, their highest total of this long, long series.

Marsh, well supported in that partnership of 97 by debutant wrist-spinner Kerry O'Keeffe (27) who, like Chappell, had benefitted from missed chances. Finally, the sequence of lower order collapses had been halted.

Marsh had also needed runs. While he most probably would have held his place for the remainder of the summer, his spot in the side and self-confidence in his ability at Test level, would have been in doubt if he had failed again.

England was 3/88 early on day three but through centuries from Brian Luckhurst (109) and Basil D'Oliveira (117) got as far as 392.

There was more trouble for Lawry during England's long road to recovery from their jittery start.

The twenty-one-year-old boyish blond O'Keeffe at that stage was thought of as a potential new Bill O'Reilly. Fast through the air for a wrist-spinner, he relied as much on bounce as turn. Luckhurst and D'Olivera in front of the best gathering of the whole summer were in some trouble against him in his first spell. He hit a length and regularly beat the bat. But Lawry refused to increase the pressure by crowding the batsmen with close-in fieldsmen. Eventually the

English pair saw out the threat and the Australian attack, minus another debutant, Queensland swing bowler Ross Duncan, lame after fourteen largely innocuous overs, again looked threadbare.

The England first innings dragged on well into the fourth day. In nearly four hours they added just 134 runs from Saturday's close of 4/258. Alan Knott batted over two hours for 19 runs. Illingworth could have been 'I-don't-care-Pierre' such was his reluctance to move the game forward.

Australia, with a lead of 101 and one down in the series, then made 1-70 in the two-hour final session. Lawry was still cancelling out the chance of defeat before any thought of victory.

In the first session on day five the Australians showed enough energy to gather 99 runs and Lawry declared at lunch with a lead of 270.

Boycott and Edrich, taking revenge for first innings failures, echoed their I-don't-care captain and batted out the entire pointless four hours. For Australia, Duncan didn't bowl and opening batsman and part time bowler Keith Stackpole sent down 13 overs while supposed number-one spinner John Gleeson was used for just three.

The banging-can protest in the outer was so loud according to *Australian Cricket* editor Eric Beecher, Illingworth's end of match interviews, obviously recorded before stumps, were ruined by the background noise.

6th Test

Although no one realised it at the time, this Test in Adelaide brought an era to a close. The last in the 1961-1971 saturation of drawn Ashes Tests, it saw Illingworth refuse the opportunity to force Australia to follow-on, the post-match sacking of Bill Lawry as player and captain of Australia and the first-time selection of Dennis Lillee in the on-again, off-again carousel of Australian fast bowlers in this series.

Lawry's problems with handling his bowling attack, especially spinners, have been documented. However, as Ian Redpath suggested, Australia's bowling stocks were thin and he did not have much to work with once Connolly and McKenzie became stale and fatigued.

Lillee was young. He bowled with genuine pace. There was no certainty then though that he would emerge from the mediocre pack as one of the best ever and spearhead Australian fast bowling for more than a decade.

Lawry, probably not knowing much about the newcomer, bowled him into a strong wind at Adelaide Oval. The captain's fellow Victorian, Alan Thomson, got the choice of ends.

Lillee picked up five wickets as England won the toss, batted and compiled 470. He out-bowled the flagging Thomson, on the second day sending down some excellent overs. England's big total still shut out Australia's chances of a win.

They had been an even more imposing 2/276 at stumps on day one. Not only was the bowling tame, but the fielding was also poor. If Boycott and Edrich's MCG 5th day 0-161 was added to the last one and two-thirds days Australia had been in the field, the score line was 2/437.

About the only fun the home side had was telling Boycott where the Adelaide dressing room was located. The Yorkshireman had thrown down his bat in disgust and stood as a double-handled tea pot at being adjudged run-out by umpire Max O'Connell. The Chappell brothers were quickest on the scene to retrieve Boycott's bat, hand it back and remind him of what his cricketing commitments were once an umpire had given him out.

It is yet another of those old incidents where it would be lovely to have the truth revealed by DRS equipment.

The brief blow-up had little real effect on the direction of match. It did show up Boycott's obsessive batting temperament and the media then questioned his suitability for captaincy honours at Test and County level. Those honours still eventually came his way, albeit briefly for England.

Stackpole made a welcome return to form as Australia began its reply after tea on day two. He was 41 out of 50 by stumps. Lawry, seemingly locked into his all-defence mode on the other hand, had struggled to eight in the ninety minutes available.

He was caught behind early the next day and his team's position became worse as the day went on. From 1/117 Australia collapsed to 235 all out. Lawry was out after twenty minutes.

The rest of his side's batting went further into its shell and began to crumble. Redpath batted nearly as long as his captain and failed to reach double figures. Greg Chappell, right back down to earth after his glorious debut, returned home to his adoring Adelaide crowd and made a duck. Peter Lever (4/49) bowling genuine outswing at a real clip ripped into the Australian middle order. In disarray at 6/163 the improving Australian tail offered some resistance adding 72 for the last four wickets.

Then Illingworth, he said at the behest of his fast-bowling

contingent, sent Boycott and Edrich out to bat again. Scoring the amount of first-wicket runs that made Hobbs and Sutcliffe legends for England on two Australian tours in the 1920s, they proceeded to put together their third consecutive century opening partnership. Boycott, avoiding personal run-out pitfalls, went on to make an unbeaten (what else?) 119 and Illingworth declared at 4/233, a lead of 468.

The England second innings lasted 51 eight-ball overs. Of those 408 deliveries, Ashley Mallett, selected as the second spinner in partnership with Johnny Gleeson, on his home ground was allocated eight by his captain, i.e. one over. The mutual cricketing respect between the two was at an all-time low.

Lawry said that Illingworth had kept the series alive by not enforcing the follow-on. But the Englishman was now the only one in a position of power where he had choice in these sorts of decisions. Just two years before, Lawry had that sort of advantage against the West Indies. Not anymore.

The Australian captain had backed himself into a negative corner and could not inspire himself or his team to get out of it. Not to the extent of playing winning or attractive cricket, anyway.

After an hour and a half of second innings resistance he hooked at a Bob Willis bouncer and, just as he had done early on the first morning of the summer to Snow, either edged or gloved a catch through to Knott. He exited the crease hoping his fellow batsmen would give him one last chance at levelling the series and retaining the Ashes back in Sydney.

Keith Stackpole and Ian Chappell did keep the English attack at bay for much of the fifth day. They scored centuries, Chappell's crucially his second in as many Tests, and with a little later help from Redpath and Walters, a docile pitch and, according to Illingworth, the inability of his leading fast bowler Snow to rouse himself sufficiently, Australia escaped with a draw.

The series was indeed alive, but as a Test cricketer, Bill Lawry wasn't.

Sections of the press knew what was going on before the two protagonists, Lawry and Ian Chappell, found out. South Australian journalist Alan "Sheffield" Shiell told Chappell of his promotion from vice-captain to captain while as previously mentioned it was Keith Stackpole who passed the word on to Lawry that he had been omitted from the team for the seventh Test in Sydney.

Lawry created confusion over how he heard the information. But both Ian Redpath and Keith Stackpole in their respective autobiographies insist they broke the news to their fellow Victorian, not, as Wikipedia and Malcolm Knox's book *The Captains,* suggests that he heard it for the first time over his car radio.

There is some confusion too over what part Lawry's letters to the Australian Cricket Board strongly criticising the scheduling, handling, payment and organisation of the lengthy twin tours of India and South Africa in 1969-70 had in his sacking.

The selectors and the members of the cricket board said Lawry's plane had left Adelaide before they had a chance to tell him of his fate. It seems to be a misguided excuse for their rude oversight.

That footage of him arriving back at Melbourne airport shows Lawry and the media knew the situation by the time he touched down.

In an interview in the *Brisbane Courier Mail* in January 2016 Neil Harvey took credit for initiating the move with his fellow selectors.

"I said to Don, 'I think now's our chance – he's gotta go – the game needs a shot in the arm and he's not the bloke to do it.' Don agreed, so we sacked him."

Harvey emphasised Lawry's poor batting form and negative approach. That surely was the clincher in making a desperate effort to change momentum in the series and retain the Ashes. Australia had gone nine Tests without a win. Lawry wasn't exactly runless but had not scored a century for 15 Tests and nearly all his good scores since early 1969 had been in second innings trying to resurrect his team from a poor position.

England had tried a similar tactic in 1926 and 1930. They replaced Carr with Chapman in the first instance and Chapman with Wyatt four years later. It worked the first time, not the second.

Lawry's removal was huge. Momentous enough for the story to feature in the opening pages of both Stackpole's *Not Just for Openers* and Chappell's *Chappelli*.

The new captain was proud to receive the honour of taking the reins at the helm of Australian cricket. He was disgusted, though, at the treatment of a man he often disagreed with, but whom he respected immensely.

"They will never get me like that," he promised.

Chappell would have liked Lawry in his team for the seventh Test in Sydney and the sacked captain would eventually finish with a better series batting average than the new man at the helm. But outside Victoria, including inside the dressing room of the

Australian team, there was a strong feeling that a change at the top was needed.

"The tone in the dressing room changed immediately when Ian Chappell took over," says Doug Walters. "There was more an attitude that we are going to play for a win and are going to go all out to achieve that. That seemed to instil a new confidence in the side.

"Before long the cricket became more enjoyable and of course it helped that some good bowlers, like Dennis Lillee, came on the scene.

"Crowds became more animated and more engaged with the Australian cricket team. They enjoyed the way we played and so bigger crowds began to take an interest and follow us."

The mould had been broken in more ways than one. Until 1971 Victoria and New South Wales had usually shared the Test captaincy. Going back to the dawn of Test cricket in 1877 Victorians who had captained Australia included legendary names such as Ian Johnson, Lindsay Hassett, Bill Woodfull, Jack Ryder, Warwick Armstrong, Hugh Trumble, Harry Trott, Percy McDonnell, Tup Scott, Jack Blackham and Tom Horan. Since Lawry's sacking, Graham Yallop, installed aged 26 during the World Series Cricket era, is the only Victorian to be crowned with the national leadership. That poorly thought-out experiment failed to last the distance of the entire 1978-79 season.

There have been none since, although many of his closest confidants suggest Shane Warne had a strong case to be promoted to the position beyond the sprinkling of ODIs where he led the side.

"To be a bit conspiratorial for a moment," says Paul Sheahan who in addition to playing 27 Tests was President of the Melbourne Cricket Club from 2011-15, "I think there might be a New South Wales cricket mafia. There are things that have gone New South Wales' way that could have gone Victoria's way but didn't.

"There's a power clique with proximity to the levers which doesn't exist in Victoria. I would be hard pressed to be convinced that it wasn't the case.

"But it is also difficult to argue that we haven't been well served by those captains from New South Wales, too."

Lawry, at Melbourne airport and hair Brylcreamed within an inch of its life, large microphones almost lost up the nostrils of that enormous nose, refused to say anything other than it was his batting form that cost him his position. He said he wished and believed Ian Chappell would do well as the new Australian captain because he had been picked when he was in good batting form, the best time to lead the side.

In the ABC 2006 DVD *Cricket in the '70s* dignified and honest, Lawry would only say, "I just would have thought after 25 Tests a Bradman would have said, look you are going to miss out tomorrow."

The comparison between Phantom's restrained reaction to very inconsiderate treatment to the behaviour of certain modern players who destroyed team spirit in dressing rooms or who still bear personal grudges for decisions taken twenty years ago, could not be more marked.

Lawry's charm and self-deprecating humour became more evident as the years passed and he became an institution behind the microphone on Australian television cricket coverage.

In my view his commentary style was far more timeless and suited to modern audiences than Ian Chappell's. Chappell still write's perceptively and his reflective thoughts can be astute. But his at-the-microphone tone of nice guys finish last, the '70s was best and me and my mates are better blokes and players than everyone else since, attitude and approach seems dated to me and many others.

Now, that is ironic.

7th Test

Like an act of God signalling the washing away the sins of the old and bringing in the fresh the clean and the new, six inches of rain fell in Sydney in the fortnight prior to the seventh Test.

Bradman took the heavenly hint and announced he was standing down as Chairman of Selectors at the end of the season.

The cleansing of Lawry, though, did not impress his fellow Victorians as much as it did the NSW contingent.

Ian Redpath said the dropping of Lawry as captain was "criminal" his dropping as player was "suicidal".

Paul Sheahan was recalled to the Australian squad for the 7th Test although he was eventually made 12th man. As well as remembering the "unusual privilege" of carrying out the drinks with none other than future knight, Colin Cowdrey, Sheahan recalls the mood of the Victorian contingent in the dressing room at the SCG.

"The game itself of course was a high tension affair on the field," Sheahan says. "But also inside the Australian dressing room there was still a lot of ill feeling amongst the Victorians; that is myself,

Stacky (Keith Stackpole) and Redders (Ian Redpath) and even Ken Eastwood, towards Bill's treatment.

"Not so much for the fact that Bill had lost the captaincy, but for the manner or the circumstances of his omission.

"I personally felt Bill was a bit of a fall-guy for the inadequacies of the people around him. He'd batted his guts out for the country and his captaincy record was not parlous.

"He took the brunt of some unfair criticism, I thought. He felt he had to carry a team and therefore he played a lot more cautiously than was his nature.

"He was actually a pretty attacking batsman when he was given his head. I remember him making a hundred in a 50-over game in a domestic final in Adelaide for Victoria and it was one of the most attacking innings that you would ever want to see.

"But he felt because he was the most experienced player with not necessarily many high quality individual players around him, he often had to dig in and play the sheet anchor role.

"No one from the Board had the courage or decency to pull Bill aside during the Adelaide Test and say, 'we are embarking on a new era and you're not part of it.'

"We all thought that was disgraceful."

Sheahan recognised quickly that Chappell's elevation would alter the tenor of the Australian cricket team.

"Ian's elevation was signalling the emergence of a new attitude to cricket by Australia," Sheahan says. "Not all of which was happily received. I think Ian rubbed a few people up the wrong way. But that was his nature.

"He was pretty competitive. His philosophy was, 'grasp the bull by the horns and fortune favours the brave'.

"And even the Australian Board were keen for us to commit to more attractive cricket. More results, more overs in an hour, more runs per over. That sort of thing."

Even those outside the Victorian group, who applauded the selection of Chappell as captain, believed his predecessor should have retained his spot in the side.

There was also a press move to recall Graham McKenzie. He had already done Australia a favour by breaking Geoff Boycott's arm in a meaningless one-day fixture between the sixth and seventh Test on an SCG green top.

Alan Thomson was left out. His replacement was not McKenzie, however. Big burly English-born left-arm quick Tony Dell got the call up. The adopted Queenslander would form with Dennis Lillee Australia's sixth different new-ball combo of the summer.

Considering fast bowlers Eric Freeman and Laurie Mayne (retired in 1970) had played Tests in South Africa early in 1970 and had not been selected in the current series, nor had 1968 Ashes and 1970 New Zealand tourist Dave Renneberg, it meant the Australian selectors had probably at no other time in history cast such a wide net in search for a Test-class fast bowler.

Chappell immediately made a statement of intent when he won the toss on the first morning at the SCG and sent England in to bat.

The wicket was damp so the move, in retrospect at least, was certainly not outrageous. Chappell's early and successful call up of Walters to the bowling crease when Lillee and Dell were immediately inaccurate and ineffective was intuitive and his use of recalled wrist-spinners Terry Jenner and Kerry O'Keeffe bore better results than one imagined might have happened if Lawry had been at the helm.

Also, Chappell, a man keen to break convention, on his first day as Test captain wore his white towelling hat while standing at slip rather than the traditional baggy green cap.

It was one of the first of what would be dozens of future non-conformation acts by the foundation-shaking South Australian.

With Jenner and O'Keeffe both taking three wickets, England were bowled out for 184 before the end of the first day. Their previous lowest total in a completed innings that summer had been 332.

Australia had also lost two wickets by stumps.

Twelve wickets had fallen in one day. Immediately, media and public interest in the actual contest was sparked.

Day two then launched it as a game that would stay in everyone's memory for all time.

The intriguing cricket and eventual tight result are reasons why the seventh Test of the 1970-71 series is often included in both vision and print compilations of *Ashes Greatest Hits.* But it is the serious crowd disturbance (or mild riot; depending on your perspective) that really elevated its profile.

In the final session, in front of a healthy Saturday crowd, as Australia struggled to build a first innings lead John Snow hit Australian No.9 batsman Terry Jenner on the crown of the head with a short-pitched delivery.

Stunned and bleeding, Jenner was assisted from the field. Umpire Rowan warned Snow for intimidatory bowling. Both the Sussex quick and his captain, Illingworth, took exception with Rowan's tone and warning and argued with the Queensland detective.

Snow, already perceived by many Australians as the villain of the series, after walking to fine-leg was accosted by a drunk spectator who lent over the fence and grabbed him by the shirt-sleeve.

"I thought about striking out until I realised he was drunk and it would have been a stupid thing to do anyway," said Snow.

Some beer bottles and cans were thrown onto the ground in the general direction of Snow and a stubborn young Bob Willis who was willing to stand in the vicinity and advise the mob of their errors of judgment. Illingworth, to a throng of boos and catcalls, then marched his team off the field.

There are iconic photos of Jenner in the act of going down from the blow, of Rowan and Illingworth arguing, of the Englishmen leaving the field and of new Test cricketers Greg Chappell and Dennis Lillee squatting in the middle of the wicket wondering what the acceptable reaction in such a situation should be.

With no precedent available, they just stayed put and watched the events unfold.

The umpires walked off too and informed Illingworth if he and his side didn't return to the field they would forfeit the match. Illingworth said they would be back as soon as the field was cleared of bottles and it was safe for his side to be out there.

The cricket world split in its opinions as to whether Illingworth and/or Rowan acted appropriately or not. Richie Benaud's view, at a distance of half a century seems as balanced as anyone's. On the still-available television commentary he criticised the open and hostile debating of Rowan's warning to Snow for short pitched bowling, but felt the English captain was entitled to take his team off the field when they were threatened by the unacceptable behaviour of unruly members of the crowd.

"In this case, I'm (usually) a backer of Illingworth, but he was behaving not like an England captain but more like the prima donna of a South American football side," Benaud said about Illingworth wagging his finger at Rowan as he revealed his thoughts on the BBC highlights package.

Current ground rules, strong penalties for invasions or transgressions, restrictions on receptacles brought into venues, and boundary ropes five metres or more inside a fence mean that in 2025 only Inspector Gadget could grab a fieldsman as Snow was by that anonymous drunken idiot in early 1971.

The events of that lovely hot sunny afternoon at the SCG were sufficiently volatile for the Test to be included in Ray Robinson's 1972 book, *The Wildest Tests* and nobody before or since relates the details any better than Sugar Ray.

Lou Rowan in *The Umpire's Story* and Illingworth *Yorkshire and Back* also give detailed and lengthy descriptions of their part in the drama, however the accounts of both are a little undermined by conflicting self-righteous bias.

From Australia's viewpoint the most significant aspect was not so much the first innings lead of 80 that they gleaned, but the three hours that Greg Chappell spent at the crease over his top-score of 65.

The 22-year-old unscrambled the batting ideas he had been offered after his Perth debut hundred. He had found a formula for constructing innings that would be the cornerstone of his brilliant career over the next dozen years.

Yet another piece of the Australian and Ashes cricketing revival had fallen into place.

If the late Saturday afternoon viewing on the ABC had been compulsive for mostly the wrong reasons, Sunday was equally riveting because of the cut and thrust of the cricketing contest.

Only a barely satisfactory 96,834 attended over the five days. Many more though would have watched the Sunday afternoon action on television.

O'Keeffe and Jenner made inroads into the English middle-order. Ian Chappell pulled a rabbit out of his white towelling hat and gave Lawry's replacement Ken Eastwood a bowl. He landed some of his left-arm wrist spin, but it was a full-toss that Keith Fletcher hit straight into Stackpole's hands at mid-wicket.

When John Hampshire top edged a sweep off O'Keeffe, captain Chappell ran from first slip behind the keeper, dived and held an exciting catch as he slid across the outfield.

In contrast to his predecessor, everything he did exuded positive energy. Whereas Lawry generally fielded at mid-on or mid-off and would stroll over or away from bowlers back to his position, Chappell after a conversation with the bowler had to jog back to first-slip, chest thrust out of his half-unbuttoned shirt.

The dismissals kept the Test on an edge. Only openers Brian Luckhurst (59) and John Edrich (57) passed the half-century mark. However, there were contributions between 15 and 47 from the rest of the batsman down to No.9. On the fourth day England again made it past three hundred (302).

Australia needed 223. If the target was reached the series scoreline yet again would finish 1-1 and the Ashes would be retained.

The home side were helped early in the chase when John Snow was put out of the match. Almost immediately, he bowled Eastwood for a duck with a yorker that made the opener hop around, looking as if fearing a broken foot.

"I inside edged the ball on to my pad and then it rolled onto the stumps," Eastwood said.

Soon after, Snow mangled the little finger of his right hand in the top of the SCG pickets.

He ran back to get under a top-edged hook by Stackpole and failed to decelerate in good time before clattering into the fence. It was just about the same spot where he had been accosted by the drunk.

Australia's leading run scorer of the summer also survived when England's best shout for lbw for the whole series was turned down. Bowler Illingworth looked to the heavens in frustration. The tourists had not had one successful lbw appeal in seven Tests!

It was probably fortunate that the umpire who rejected the appeal was Tom Brooks, not Lou Rowan.

With Snow out of action and the wicket taking some spin, Illingworth (3-39) himself filled the breach. He had Redpath caught at short leg and eventually bowled Stackpole (67) around his legs, sweeping. The final morning which began with Australia five wickets down and exactly 100 runs from victory, he drifted the ball past an advancing Greg Chappell and had him neatly stumped by Alan Knott.

At the last gasp Australia's tail, its Achilles heel for several summers, again surrendered meekly. On that sunny fifth morning fives wickets fell for just 37 runs.

When Terry Jenner, head sore but intact, was caught at silly mid off by Fletcher from Deadly Derek Underwood Australia were all out for 160.

England had won the seventh Test by 62 runs and had taken the series 2-0. The Ashes had changed hands the first time since 1958-59.

Here, finally, after nine and half years and so many, many hours of either occasional one-sided results or games that ran into obstacles, roadblocks and dead-ends was an Ashes Test match to really savour and retain in the memory for mostly good cricketing things.

Illingworth was chaired from the field on the shoulders of John Edrich and John Hampshire. His achievement best summed up by, rather than words, the photo of Snow and Boycott both with their arms in slings on the ground post-match.

For Australia, forfeiting the Ashes was like losing an ancient relative. There was sadness that they had gone, but the recent months had shown their time was nigh.

Ian Chappell had failed to back up his hundred in Melbourne and Adelaide with significant run-scoring contributions in the Sydney crunch Test. He had, however, received a big tick for his captaincy and catching.

"There's no doubt Ian did a really good job of galvanising the side and getting them to pull together in a very short space of time as a unit in that Test," says Paul Sheahan.

Chappell and Illingworth, according to Brian Chapman in T*he Guardian*, still agreed "the concept of the Ashes is outdated, and each series should be contested in its own right."

Many others were facing a more questionable cricketing future than Chappell and Illingworth. Australian selectors and the cricketing executive have always reacted unfavourably to home Ashes series losses. 1970-71 was no exception.

The fates of Bill Lawry, Graham McKenzie and Alan Connolly have been discussed here. Ken Eastwood, Alan Thomson and Ross Duncan (despite one game v Rest of the World in '71-72) would play no more official Test cricket.

From Illingworth's Test heroes of that summer only three, Cowdrey, Shuttleworth and Willis, failed to play even one Test in the 1972 Ashes series. All would again be selected for England at some stage after Sydney 1971.

CHAPTER THIRTEEN

1972 ASHES; WHAT A BEAUTIFUL THING

There are several landmarks that might be considered the time when the Beatles no longer could be thought of as an entity.

For most practical purposes it was when Paul McCartney announced he was leaving in 1970. Others have even suggested it occurred when the band stopped playing live in 1966. Joe Strummer shouted on the timeless 1979 Clash song 'London Calling', "Phoney Beatlemania has bitten the dust." He had a point.

Then there's 1980; the date of John Lennon's frightening, mindless murder.

My son, Ben, also a musician, says maybe it was 1975 after the final Apple album, George Harrison's *Extra Texture*, was released. Ben says that George's solo work until *Extra Texture* is also thought to contain the most Beatle-like sound and production.

In my view 1972 is the strongest candidate. For that was the year that three Beatles failed to release a solo studio album and the one that did, John Lennon, received a big critical kick up the backside.

Sometime in New York City does have at least three tracks that sound great, but there are too many inaccessible Yoko Ono songs interspersed and Lennon's lyrics are obviously and blandly political.

McCartney was already chastened by his 1971 release *Wings Wild Life*, some of which now seems really good spontaneous fun to me – and his lame single 'Mary had a Little Lamb'.

Harrison carried credibility over from his revered *All Things*

Must Pass triple-disc classic, but concentrated on the human rights issues in Bangladesh and released no new studio album.

None, including Ringo, were finished as artists (Paul and Ringo, into their eighties, are still putting out new songs at the time of writing). In 1972, though, the Beatles as a band or as solo artists in the eyes of the public and music critics bottomed out.

It is mostly coincidence that that was the same year the Ashes captured the imagination of the English populous and the cricket world in general in a way unseen since 1961. The photo of Mick Jagger carrying two pints at The Oval Test back to his seat did seem to indicate that Ashes cricket had grown up somewhat and had crossed a youth divide.

Rolling Stones drummer Charlie Watts and then bass player Bill Wyman were also big cricket fans. Unlike the Beatles, the Stones were going from strength to strength in the early seventies with the release of two classic albums *Sticky Fingers* and *Exile on Main Street*. Their public profile was bigger than ever and even more prominent than the Beatles at that time.

Eric Clapton and Elton John are two more rock/pop megastars who were at their creative and popular peak in the early to mid '70s who also had no inhibitions in showing their passion for cricket.

As previously mentioned, that rekindling of interest doesn't show up in the attendance in the 1st Test at Manchester. The thirty-eight thousand aggregate is actually a lower figure than in 1968, although television ratings figures are unknown.

The people were there in big numbers at Lord's as usual and then as the series became such a fluctuating classic the grounds were filled at Nottingham, Leeds and at the Oval in South London.

And they were entertained for their time and effort by games that, apart from Trent Bridge, brought about a result. The wonderfully entertaining Oval Test was in doubt right to the second session of the final sixth day.

In another symbol of the times Australia's tense successful fourth innings run chase was televised live by satellite into Australian homes by the ABC. It was absorbing viewing.

Paul Sheahan's unbroken match-clinching sixth-wicket partnership of 71 with Rod Marsh delighted the whole country.

As the tension grew, Sheahan had a breakout moment against his old tormentor, Underwood.

It could be seen as yet another symbol of the old being thrown out for the new.

"I had probably reached a score in the late teens," Sheahan says. "And I thought, if there's anything around leg stump I'm going to try sweeping. I got one on leg stump and I swept it.

"It hit flush in the middle of the bat and it went for four. And I looked up and Underwood's eyes were more open that usual with a look of 'how did he do that?' And then I got another ball on leg stump past mid-on for four. After that he didn't bowl nearly as well to me.

"To level that series after all the brilliant cricket and ups and downs was a great result.

"In a lot of those contests there are crucial moments and if you happen to seize them things will fall your way. If you don't you will lose the initiative and it will be very hard to wrest it back again."

Only one tour book was commissioned. *The Ashes 1972* by John Arlott was reviewed as lacking in much substance by one reviewer.

But I loved it. I asked for it for my 16th birthday, received it joyously and still have it and treasure it. I even swoon at the sweet smell of its old pages.

Arlott captured the mood of the games and conveyed the enthusiasm I wanted to hear.

He wrote in the epilogue to the book, "The England-Australia Tests of 1972, completely unpredictable in their course, provided constant surprise and suspense. This was quite remarkable. Anyone who denies that some previous series have been monotonous, defensive and ultimately pointless, must be unreasonably partisan, thick-witted or blinkered. Here however was a rubber of games which was played out at full competition without acrimony. The major series was enjoyable, exciting and often fiercely stressful to watch."

What must have frustrated the players from the 1960s was that for the first time since 1961 an Ashes series in England also had the benefit of none of the games losing significant amounts of time to rain.

This time *Wisden* editor Norman Preston responded to the summer's entertainment by naming four Australian players as "Cricketers of the Year."

Budding champions Lillee and Greg Chappell established their prowess with clinch performances on the big Ashes stage, Keith Stackpole, leading run scorer for the whole series and on the tour and Bob Massie for his one amazing Test-match haul of 16 wickets, were all recognised. They were joined, an almost belated choice, by Snow who took 50% more wickets than the next best English bowler.

No English batsman was nominated. Not one made a century over the five Test matches.

Then there were Patrick Eagar's photographs. The dust jacket cover of John Arlott's tour book is his vibrant colour shot of Marsh hoisting the ball into the air after catching Alan Knott at Old Trafford. The slips are doing star jumps and Lillee, on the back side of the dust jacket, is pirouetting in mid-air, his mop of black hair swirling like an energetic rock guitarist.

It is a telling comparison to John Gleeson's studious forward prod on the cover of the 1968 equivalent book.

Eagar's photos are another significant aspect of Test cricket's revival in the early 1970s. With grounds in England now opened up to freelance photographers rather than just monopolised by an agency, Eagar could exhibit his skill on better equipment. The result was the best cricket photography seen to that time.

Son of the former Hampshire CCC captain, Desmond, his intuition for the game led to the players in their pomp being brought closer and more clearly to the public than ever before.

His timing with the emergence of this engaging group of cricketers at the same time could not have been better. It was beneficial to him, the cricketers and the game itself.

"Rather than a long scene with a whole group of players in the distance," Paul Sheahan says. "You got real close ups which captured the essence of the emotion that was being displayed at the time, with photographers like Patrick Eagar, who was an outstanding artist with his camera."

The images have not aged at all and look as fresh today as they did in all sorts of publications in 1972.

Embarrassingly when David Frith introduced me to Patrick in the media lunchroom during the Ashes Test at Cardiff in 2009 I gushed about how strong an impression his 1972 photos made on me.

When I singled out a photo of Ian Chappell at the Oval clipping Derek Underwood through mid-wicket in *The Cricketer Winter Annual* of 1972, he just looked at me in puzzlement. He probably wondered why that one out of the millions and millions he has taken was so special.

Ian Chappell's own tour book *Tigers Among Lions* was released a little later. It has cheaper production values than Arlott's book and is a little light on detail. It is nevertheless a totally justifiable attempt to cash in on the newfound interest in the Ashes. It also could be considered a precursor to all the tour and season diaries written by future Australian Test captains Michael Clarke, Steve Waugh and Ricky Ponting that sold by the truckload in the '90s and early 2000s.

In 1972 I compiled another scrapbook of scores and photos cut daily from newspapers.

It's in my house somewhere. I don't have to find it to remember many of the dozens of photos of tour matches and the Tests squeezed in loosely between the pages of an exercise book originally labelled and covered in clear plastic to be used for listing Form Three German vocabulary and verb conjugations.

There's Bob Massie holding his side and looking forlorn as he is about to leave the playing group after straining a muscle in his side just a couple of overs in against the MCC at Lord's.

Graeme Watson, off balance as he cuts and edges Geoff Arnold at Old Trafford. Ian Chappell's desperate grimace as he hooks riskily and hard at Lord's. Basil D'Oliveira being trapped lbw by Lillee at Trent Bridge.

And the shot of Ian Chappell mid-leap about to catch John Hampshire at first slip in the second innings of the 5th Test at the Oval is another clear in the mind's eye.

Then in 1988 came the release of the BBC VHS *The Ashes '72: Fast and Furious.*

The whole magnificent series comes alive again in a two-hour highlights package.

The colour looks a little watery and the images are hardly HD, yet the merit of the action is obvious. This was one of the first BBC releases when their archive was opened up for tapes to be sold to the public. They made a great choice, although this particular decision was probably a very easy one.

And though the colour is hardly HD quality, the cricket watching television public, in England at least, was seeing the game's images in a more vibrant life like way. As it was in the social world outside cricket, the grey scales were falling away.

Australia, never in a hurry on these matters, had to wait another year or two for colour television.

Lillee bounding in and hitting Boycott on the elbow on the first freezing morning at Manchester, the hopeless English slips-catching matched by Australian batting incompetence in the first innings and repeated, Stackpole excepted, in the second until Marsh led a belated six-hitting assault.

Australia holding everything in the slips at Lord's, Greg Chappell countering the brilliance of John Snow in upright classic fashion for a dream century. Derek Underwood doing all sorts of tricks on a controversial Leeds pudding wicket as Australian batsmen become more and more disillusioned. "A shocker" as Paul Sheahan puts it.

Then the sun-drenched Oval providing compensation with that pulsating last innings chase of 242 as Ian Chappell's team meted out justice and tied the rubber, not 1-1 thank goodness, but 2-2.

Illingworth bemoaned both English losses on fate turning against him. It was the freakish overcast weather at Lord's on the Saturday that allowed Bob Massie to swing the ball so late.

Illingworth said it rained everywhere else in London apart from at NW8 and each time the ball landed it left a green "slur mark" on the wicket surface.

The reality was that it was overcast when Australia batted on the Friday and on the Saturday morning when they added a further 107 for their last five wickets.

Then he couldn't believe the fifth Test was to be played over six days when the Ashes had been decided. Which gave Australia enough time to win by five wickets.

Illingworth, who turned 40 during the series, twisted his ankle on the fifth evening when bowling and could not spin Australia out on the final day.

He is the only one to raise such excuses. He denies any skulduggery was behind the one true controversy of the series when the Leeds pitch for the crucial 4th Test was presented as devoid of grass. The fuserium (fungus) fiasco where only the grass on the wicket was destroyed by disease, none anywhere else on the square, and the selection of soft wicket specialist Derek Underwood was a coincidence too hard to bear for most Australians.

Illingworth, who top scored in the match with 57, claimed it was nothing more than a regular English slow, low turner. That it sucked out the life of the Australian fast bowlers was mere coincidence, according to the person who benefitted the most from that distinctive preparation at the venue that was his home ground for 20 years.

The Australian team did not publicly complain and it must be said the three-day match did add variety to the series. Apart from the flat pitch at Trent Bridge, ironically played in the best weather of the summer, there was a green top at Old Trafford, conditions that favoured swing bowling at Lord's, the fuserium pitch at the Headingley and the perfect six-day pitch at the Oval. Every game provided something different. It was absorbing from start to finish.

In my lifetime the Ashes series of 1972 stands alongside 2005, 2019 and 2023. All are like this long beautiful soft-drug trip. Or what I imagine a soft-drug trip would be like.

"We had an unbelievable series in 1972," says Paul Sheahan. "The cricket was tense, enthralling and competitive with lots of brilliant highlights.

"The changes in the image of the team came out through changes in social context but also the change in the different personalities of the members of the 1972 team.

"There was a liberation of social morays. We had just come out of Vietnam and all that sort of stuff. People were thumbing their nose at authority.

"Personally, now, I'm not sure all of that liberation was such a good idea."

Ian Chappell said in 1993 that he was pleased with what his

team achieved in 1972 because they matched England who were then the best side in the world.

There was no official measure in 1972. England was a solid unit between 1969 and 1972. South Africa were better, but their isolation had begun so Chappell was just about right in his assessment.

He was also right that he had a side that was ready to assume the mantle of world No.1 and a 2-2 result in England suggested progress was being made towards that objective.

Also crucial was the forming of a team nucleus of top-quality players with genuine and varied charisma.

Masculine-committed '70s-style rebel Ian Chappell, his more austere upright brother oozing classical movement and A+ grade batting talent, cheerful dashing man of the people Doug Walters, strong hairy teddybear-like Rod Marsh and the racing black stallion of an express fast bowler Dennis Lillee; there was someone there for everyone to love, male or female.

England too, but more slowly, was changing the dynamic and image of their side. While Illingworth, John Edrich, Brian Luckhurst and Derek Underwood could fit in any team photo between 1947 and 1972 there were a couple of players who looked like they belonged in the '70s.

John Snow had grown a genuinely heavy black mop of hair. Mean, moody and magnificent, the fast bowler was always at his best against Australia. He was rebellious, wrote poetry and turned ladies' heads wherever he went.

Then in 1972 Tony Greig became a fixture in the English side. The six-foot-seven South African-born blond oozed on-field cricketing aggression with his every step and facial expression.

He was, and intended to be, a very marketable cricketer. He shook the image of the England team by its collar. In 1972 it was by small steps. Later those steps would grow massively.

By the time Australia welcomed England in 1974-75 every playing component was in place. The Ashes was again a joyously anticipated event. When 77,000 turned up on Boxing Day for day one of the 3rd Test at the MCG, and 250,000 attended over the five days, any thought that The Urn should be smashed with Maxwell's Silver or anyone else's hammer and thrown out in the rubbish was well forgotten.

Although a draw, the only one for the six-match Australia-dominated series, the match had a cliff hanging climax.

An Australian sporting institution, the Boxing Day Test, was established.

Even my mother and sister, non-cricket fans both, attended with dad and me. We had to sit on the concrete terraces of the standing room area in the old 1956-built Olympic Stand.

It was hard on the posterior and occasionally the gentlemen behind us lost control of their oft-purchased drinking receptacles. We had to be aware of the occasional sticky liquid steam flowing through us.

At least we were in the shade.

Anglo-Australian Test cricket would have a few more ups and downs attendance-wise in the '80s due to World Series Cricket, clustered retirements, the popularity of 50-over Internationals and top players being banned for touring South Africa with rebel teams.

The preponderance of draws and negativity never returned, though. No series since 1975 has had more draws than results.

In the '90s the Ashes crowds grew again and have remained in great numbers to this day. The official Ashes record attendance of 91,112 was recorded at the Boxing Day Test of 2013. Tickets to Ashes Tests in England cost hundreds of pounds yet the first three days are always sold out. It may shock some people to find out this was occurring pre-Bazball.

And ditching The Urn is never mentioned.

BIBLIOGRAPHY

John Arlott, *The Ashes 1972* (Pelham Books 1972)
Ken Barrington, *Playing It Straight* (Stanley Paul 1966)
Denzil Batchelor, *The Test Matches of 1964* (Epworth Press 1964)
Richie Benaud, *Spin Me A Spinner* (Hodder and Stoughton 1963)
Ian Chappell, *Chappelli* (Hutchinson 1976)
Ian Chappell, *Tigers Among Lions* (Investigator Press 1972)
John Clarke, *The Challenge Renewed* (Stanley Paul 1963).
John Clarke, *England in Australia* (Stanley Paul 1966)
Mike Coward, *The Chappell Years* (ABC Books 2002)
Colin Cowdrey, *The Incomparable Game* (Hodder and Stoughton 1970)
Colin Cowdrey, *M.C.C.* (Hodder and Stoughton 1976)
Alan Davidson, *Fifteen Paces.* (Souvenir Press1963)
Phil Derriman, *The Grand Old Ground* (Cassell Australia 1981)
Ted Dexter, *Ted Dexter Declares* (Stanley Paul 1966),
John Edrich, *Runs In the Family* (Stanley Paul 1969)
Matthew Engel ed. *The Guardian Book of Cricket* (Pavilion 1986)
Tom Goodman & A.G.Moyes, *With the MCC in Australia 1962-63* (Angus and Robertson 1963)
Tom Graveney, *Tom Graveney on Cricket* (Muller 1965),
Tom Graveney, *Cricket Over Forty* (Pelham Books 1970),
Wally Grout, *My Countrys Keeper* (Pelham Books 1965)
Gideon Haigh, *The Summer Game* (Text Melb 1997)
Neil Hawke, *Bowled Over* (Rigby 1982)
Simon Hughes, *Crickets Greatest Rivalry-A History of the Ashes in 10 Matches* (Cassell Illustrated 2013)
Ray Illingworth, *Spinners Wicket* (Stanley Paul 1968)
Ray Illingworth, *Yorkshire and Back* (Queen Anne Press 1980)
Bill Lawry, *Run-Digger* (Souvenir Press 1966)
Ken Mackay, *Slasher Opens Up* (Pelham 1964)
Ken Mackay, *Quest for the Ashes* (Pelham Books 1966)

Alan McGilvray, *Captains Of The Game* (ABC Books 1992)
Norm ONeill, *Ins and Outs* (Pelham Books1964)
Ian Redpath , *Always Reddy* (Garry Sparke 1976).
Ray Robinson, *The Wildest Tests* (Pelham Books 1972)
Lou Rowan, *The Umpires Story* (Jack Pollard Pty Ltd 1972)
Bob Simpson, *Captains Story* (Stanley Paul 1966)
Bob Simpson, *The Australians In England 1968* (Stanley Paul 1968)
John Snow, *Cricket Rebel* (Hamlyn 1976),
Keith Stackpole, *Not Just for Openers* (Stockwell Press 1974)
E.W.Swanton, *As I Said At The Time* (Collins Willow 1983)
Fred Titmus, *My Life In Cricket* (John Blake 2005)
Huw Tuberville, *The Toughest Tour* (Aurum 2010)
Ray Webster, *First-Class Cricket In Australia* Volume 2 1945-46 to 1976-77 (Self published 1997)
E.M. Wellings, *Dexter verses Benaud* (Bailey Bros & Swifen Ltd 1963)
E.M. Wellings, *Simpsons Australians* (Robert Hale Ltd 1964)
R.S.Whitingtons, *Captains Outrageous* (Stanley Paul 1972)

Wisden Cricketer's Almanack:1961 1964 1965 1967 1969 1971 1973 2000

ABC Cricket Book: 1962-63, 1964, 1965-66, 1968, 1970-71, 1972
The Cricketer International various issues 1962-1972, December 2017 edition
Australian Cricket various issues 1968-72, Yearbook 1971
Australian Cricket Society magazine Pavilion 2011
Aust Cricket Heroes No.6 (Universal magazines)
Cricket Tourguide 2010-11 (Unversal Magazines 2010)
Cornhill Insurance Test Series Six Test Programme 1993; ECB
Official Programme First npower Ashes Test Match 2009; ECB
Official Programme Second npower Ashes Test Match 2009; ECB
ACS Pavilion 2011, 2014, 2020 editions, ed. Ken Piesse

Cricket In the '60s BBC VHS
The Ashes 1972: Fast and Furious BBC VHS 1988
World of Cricket No.4 TCCB VHS 1993
ABC *Winds of Change:Cricket in the '60s* ABC;2006 dvd
ABC 2006 *The Chappell Era: Cricket in the '70s* ABC;2002 dvd

AFTERWORD

Lying half-conscious on the cold hard concrete floor of the causeway at the back of the Players Stand at Kardinia Park being cared for by paramedics I weakly whispered, "Is that blood?"

My own memories of attending Ashes Tests in the 1970s at the MCG are dominated by the brilliance of Australian fast bowlers such as Dennis Lillee, Jeff Thomson and Rodney Hogg and also of Rod Marsh and the Chappell brothers catching edged cricket balls travelling so fast you could not see them from the outer with the naked eye.

They would then throw the ball as high as the rooftop of the packed, noisy, beer-drenched and sunburnt old Southern Stand in celebration.

In these years my own playing commitments and the cost of supporting a young family restricted my attendance to one day per match.

Comprehensive coverage by ABC TV, books, magazines and newspapers partially compensated.

Opportunities in the eighties and early nineties then took my passion to a new level.

In 1990-91, for the first time, I managed to attend all five days of the Ashes Test at the MCG. I savoured the ups and downs of a game which on paper was won easily by Australia by 8 wickets. But the fortunes of both sides had fluctuated and the result was in doubt until post-lunch on day five.

I understood then the total satisfaction of witnessing the whole intricate cricket journey.

In January 1983 my wife Chris, and I made it out of Geelong to Sydney. Coincidence of coincidences it was the same time as the 5th Test of the 1982-83 Ashes series.

Chris gave me permission to travel from Cronulla to Moore Park on day three. Immediately I entered the ground and walked around to the gap between the old Hill and the Brewongle Stand I knew I had a new love.

David Gower and Derek Randall were trading cover drives. The big crowd were buzzing. And the intimacy of the outer to the cricket in the middle surpassed the MCG.

Michael Slater once told me how both venues and occasions were special. The electricity from the towering MCG filled stands almost lifting you off the ground as you walked to the centre on Boxing Day, followed barely a week later by the SCG with its engaged and knowledgeable crowd close enough for individual faces to feature to the players.

The backdrop of the historic Members and Ladies Stands smacked me in the face with delight. I have been back 17 more times including five more Ashes Tests. The excitement has never wavered.

Thankfully I missed that 2010-11 SCG disaster. Instead, I went to Adelaide. With Australia belted by an innings it was also a hard-watch. But the Adelaide Oval wasn't to blame. Pretty then, impressive now, the sense of festival and the link to the city centre makes the Test at the Adelaide Oval another perpetual lure. Twelve Tests including three for the Ashes being the current attendance count.

In 1989 with pennies saved and teachers' Long Service Leave available Chris and I journeyed to the UK and Europe for the first time.

Again, there was an Ashes-calendar happy coincidence. But the cricket had to fit in with the once-in-a-lifetime travel. So, it was limited to day four in the first Test at Leeds and days two and three and first session of day four in the second Test at Lord's.

Lord's!

Okay, forget the MCG, SCG, Gabba, WACA, Bellerive and Adelaide Oval, or Headingley, Trent Bridge, Edgbaston, Old Trafford, The Oval and Cardiff. Each and every one is wonderful.

But there is only one Lord's. I see what Keith Miller was getting at. Beyond wonderful, it is my heaven.

If the sun shines and Australia are dominating, that is.

It was and they did on Saturday, June 24th, 1989. One-nil up but not holding the Ashes they were chasing England's 286. Australia began day three on 6-276. In the better position, but not yet dominant.

By this time I had occasional-Media Accreditation so I sat in the Press Box.

New to me, that in itself was a fascination. In the back row with no deadline hanging over me, I listed in awe, then gave up so numerous were they, the playing and cricket writing legends passing through the old tiered musty room atop the now demolished and replaced Warner Stand.

Geoff Boycott went past and asked if I had a pencil. When I timidly held up a Biro, Boycott did his best Mr Pitt of *Seinfeld* impression and said, "No, not a biro, a pencil! It has to be a pencil!" And followed up with a piercing glare as if I were a Yorkshire bowler sending down a succession of full tosses and long hops.

If that was slightly intimidating the form of Allan Border's side in front of a gradually melting NW8 full house more than compensated.

First with Merv Hughes and Trevor Hohns then with a belligerent Geoff Lawson, Steve Waugh backed up his Leeds 177 with 152, both knocks not out and filled with clean sweet strokes on both sides of the wicket. Australia, labelled pre-tour the weakest ever, roared their way to 528.

Terry Alderman trapped Graham Gooch lbw third ball of England's second innings. Ready to condemn the umpire, the English tabloid press contingent tipped over chairs and noisily crowded underneath the press box TV replay screen for confirmation the Aussies had been cheating again, only to almost immediately return to their seats disconsolate. The BBC were on strike and only had a camera operating from the Pavilion end, the wrong one to judge the accuracy or otherwise of the lbw decision by Dickie Bird.

Soon after, Lawson neatly removed Chris Broad's off stump. England limped to stumps on 3-58.

It was the most amazingly fulfilling day of my cricket-watching life. I kept looking at the clock on the side wall of the press box. I wanted it – and time – to stop.

After play I just wandered around the ground a little. The sun remained proud but was softening its impact in the evening sky. Graham Garth McKenzie chatted to a few people on the steps leading from the seats up from the fence at the Nursery End in the Compton/Edrich stand.

I stood and stared for a moment at the man who as a 20-year-old had been a match-winning fast bowling star on debut at this very ground 28 years previous. He was the last of the Test legends whom I had come to within touching distance that day between 11.00am and 6.30pm. Too starry-eyed, I failed to ask any of them for their autograph.

It was hard to leave.

I desperately wanted to accost some significant MCC official and plead with him.

"Please! Please! Please! Bring them all back. I need some more!"

Two afternoons later I was on the tube train to Heathrow Airport looking forlorn as the city of London skyline disappeared into the eastern horizon.

Chris looked at my sunken expression and placed her hand on my shoulder.

"Don't worry you'll be back," she offered.

She didn't know how right she was. At times to her mild chagrin, we have been back, many, many times. For cricket watching, cricket playing, cricket coaching (eleven summer school terms of that) and classroom teaching. Both Southend-on-Sea and Bath feel like second homes.

Between 1986-87 and 2021-22 I saw at least one day live of every Ashes series home and away, except for 1993.

When Shane Warne took his hat-trick at the MCG, I was there. When Darren Gough took his hat-trick at the SCG, I was there. When Steve Waugh completed his resurrection final-ball-of-the-day century at the SCG, I was there. When Billy Bowden understandably but incorrectly gave Michael Kasprowicz out and England won by two runs at Edgbaston, I was there. When

Shane Warne claimed his 700th Test wicket at the MCG, I was there. When Ashton Agar on debut made 98 batting at No.11 at Trent Bridge, I was there. When Steve Smith made twin centuries in his first Test back from Sandpapergate suspension at Edgbaston, I was there. Then when he was cleaned up by a Jofra Archer bouncer at Lord's next Test, I was there. And I was there when Scott Boland took 6-7 and became an instant, statue worthy, MCG icon.

As the old prisoner in the Roman cell in *The Life of Brian* would say, "You lucky, lucky bastard."

I was also meant to be there when Alex Carey ruptured a relationship between two teams and two countries by running out Jonny Bairstow at Lord's. But I wasn't.

Geelong were due to play Melbourne at Kardinia Park on the evening of Thursday, June 22nd 2023, six days before the Lord's Ashes Test. I was scheduled to fly out to Heathrow on the Saturday, June 24th.

My sister-in-law who usually sits with Chris at games couldn't go. Despite a horrible weather forecast I agreed to use the free seat.

Another consideration was that six days previous I had a gastroscopy. During the procedure I was having mutated cells that threatened to become cancerous removed.

I told the gastroenterologist of my exciting travel plans.

He promised to be careful and when I awoke from my heavy sedation he assured me he had scraped off just a very small, fingernail-sized growth that was non-cancerous and that it wouldn't affect my travel plans in any way.

I had a few days of soft diet and felt slightly under the weather, but well enough, I thought, to watch my approximately 800th footy match at KP.

During the 2nd quarter an umpire whom I'd had problems with previously made decisions against Geelong right in front of me near the boundary line in the forward pocket.

I felt it was my duty to advise him that he needed to review the competence of his decision making. And being 20 rows back I had to raise my voice significantly so that he could hear the wisdom of my suggestions.

It's fair to say I may have overstretched my vocal capacity and emotion. My voice unexpectedly trailed off and my heart rate was noticeably higher than normal.

Frustratingly, I don't believe he followed my advice for the remainder of the match, but Geelong played better after half time.

Intermittent showers and a freezing wind made me question my sanity in attending, but the thought of lovely balmy summer England and the Ashes only a few days hence sustained me.

Or so I thought.

At three quarter time I stood up to stretch and breathe deeply but I had to sit down again feeling lightheaded.

Again, I thought it was nothing significant and was pleased that a last-quarter goalscoring burst saw the Cats to victory.

With Chris, I departed immediately and briskly after the final siren to circulate some blood to my extremities and beat the exiting crowd. Except at that moment there wasn't quite enough blood in my veins and arteries for me to circulate. At the top of the stairs in the causeway, with people all around, down I went.

Chris said I was out for about 20 seconds. When I regained

consciousness I was told to stay where I was. A passing doctor took my pulse. He reassured Chris it was okay.

Four different St Johns ambulance people asked me if I had been drinking. I hadn't, except for a half time hot chocolate. I didn't think they meant that.

Then I felt nauseous and vomited. I thought I must have brought up what I ate before the game at home. It might have been. But it was also a litre of blood. My oesophagus had sprung a bloody leak and it drizzled into my stomach. Blood apparently has two possible exits from the stomach. Mine came back up out of my mouth.

I calmly wondered if I was dying but felt no pain and thought if this was the finish it was better than the exit and future of my older siblings. One had already died from early onset Alzheimer's, another was in serious cognitive decline from it. Anything was better than that.

And I knew my Ashes trip was a goner.

I was meant to chaperon an Ashes-in-England uninitiated close mate. Craig, taking a different flight the day after me, was in tears when Chris opened our front door to him. He had just been told the bad news. He only boarded the plane at his wife's insistence.

A novice with English sporting crowds he shrank and cringed at their anger at Lord's after the Bairstow run-out incident. Our mutual ex-pat friend Bill sitting next to him using my ticket, was far braver in standing up to the most irrational overtly nationalistic virulent local behaviour.

The stretcher in the ambulance that took me to emergency at Geelong hospital was still warm. It was the crew's second visit that evening to Kardinia Park. They had also taken Cats star forward

Jeremy Cameron to hospital just over an hour earlier after he had been concussed by of all people, teammate Gary Rohan.

Chris, bless her, at my urging took a signed medical certificate from the hospital to the travel agent and with minutes to spare I received a credit.

Still seedy from the medical incident I used that flight credit to visit friends in London and Southend-on-Sea in September. There was not much cricket left. I got to see one day of the County Championship at Canterbury.

I also watched soccer at Craven Cottage, Loftus Road, the Olympic Stadium and The New Den. At the latter, Millwall's ground, I extended my knowledge of the force and decency of language abuse needed to properly castigate umpires/referees.

As great as it was, the Ashes 2023 is not on my viewing re-visit radar. Missing it still hurts.

Hopefully 2025-26 will be almost as good. The atmosphere inevitably sensational and England arrive believing they have a genuine chance of winning down under for the first time in 15 years.

The sense of anticipation is undiminished satisfaction guaranteed. The prospect of an addition to that list of my greatest live sporting moments and memories already creating saliva and a flutter in the tummy.

Then again, if Australia smash England 5-0 once more, I will probably enjoy that, too.

A NOTE FROM THE AUTHOR

Why on earth does the world need yet another cricket book on the Ashes? There are dozens of them; big and small, long and short, from the sublime to the ridiculous. They pop up prior to every Australian tour of England and every English tour of Australia. Some are well written and produced and entertaining, others just repeat the same stories that have been told before. On the shelves of a cricket book collector these Best of the Ashes volumes could take up a whole section themselves.

So why did I have to write this damned thing? The core of this book is about the most criticised sequence of Ashes contests of all time.

Well, the urge to tell the story of a generally wonderful sporting contest seemingly self-destructing was compelling.

There is much to celebrate from the 1960s.

Here are two of my favourites.

As this book reveals, with the Beatles at its hub, pop-rock music developed such a golden iconic era that half a century on many of the songs and albums of the time are still embraced by the young with a passion.

And the blossoming of sports telecasting entranced and captured me in my youth.

I still spend a large part of everyday watching some sort of footage, live or otherwise of Test cricket or AFL. That began for me in the 1960s. Not so many of our young folk follow me into this historic area, but my romantic attachment to classic AFL matches such as the HSV 7 telecast of the 1966 and 1967 Grand Finals and footage of the ABC's coverage 1968-69 Australia v West Indies series and the 1970-71 Ashes series rekindles the joy of a happy childhood.

But I guess the main reason this story needed to be told is my continuing frustration with hearing insistent repetition of glib generalisations about Test cricket's imminent demise. The on-going trumpeting "the end is nigh" by supposed experts in high cricketing places, the media and at times in the outer around me at various cricket grounds is completely misplaced in Australia and England.

In the 1960s Test cricket in Australia and England at least was on far shakier ground than currently. Here is a simple non-Ashes example of the current ignorance.

Day one attendance at the Australia v India Test in 2024 at the MCG, 87,242.

Day one attendance at the Australia v India Test in 1967 at the MCG, 12,688.

Who of the doomsayers knows this simple fact? None, I believe.

Those not at the MCG on December 30th 1967 may have listened to the Test on the radio. But only the post-tea session in Melbourne was televised on the ABC.

So, it is not as if people stayed at home and watched on television instead.

Ashes cricket in the 1960s was being slated left, right and centre. Numerous players, critics and even administrators were so frustrated with the sequence of stalemates that the clarion call was for the whole idea of the Ashes to be scrapped.

I can't find any evidence that it was voted as possible policy at the Cricket Board of Australia or the Test and County Cricket Board or MCC level. But Bradman did not initiate a meeting with the players to give them a pre-Ashes rev-up in 1965 purely off his own initiative. It must have been a response to serious concerns at Board level.

These Tests were played by great cricketers, as good and talented as those of any era. As men, now in their 70s and 80s and some now sadly passed, they were brilliant to talk to, great characters and genuinely fine people who believed what they were doing in the 1960s was in the best interests of their country and national cricket team. They were paid poorly and received extensive criticism. Yet there is no bitterness or regret. The destiny of the Ashes governed everything.

Captain in two Ashes Tests, contests which constituted more than 50% of his 29-match career and regular vice-captain to Bob Simpson, Brian Booth was a charming man with strong Christian beliefs and impeccable ethics. He was a stylish stroke maker whose skills as an Olympic hockey player is evident from film of his leg-side hits and sweeps against the English off-spinners. Booth summed up the feelings of thousands of Australians and indeed Englishmen to these time-honoured matches.

"As an Australian player you always had the dream of playing against England," Booth said. "I played a lot of unofficial Ashes Tests in my backyard before I played in a real one, and England didn't win any of them. I think these games are part of our history, part of our culture, part of our heritage. If I had a choice, regardless of what the standard of the two teams might be, I would rather play in a Test match against England."

And the five series under scrutiny did contain a sprinkling of absorbing contests and exciting performances. The Brisbane Test of 1962-63 was a gripping game, Headingley 1964 lay in the balance for much of its duration, there was no shortage of thrilling batting at Melbourne in the 2nd Test of 1965-66 and both Sydney Tests in 1970-71 provided more than their share of thrills and spills.

And no Test ever had a more nerve shredding climax than the Oval Test of 1968.

However, even Richie Benaud, rightly respected and loved as player, captain and commentator, the man who received so many plaudits for his part in leading Australia in the Tied Test series against the West Indies in 1960-61 and the tour of England in 1961, could not bear the thought of surrendering the Ashes at home 18 months later. Where necessary, he compromised his attacking instincts and shut up shop to ensure they were not lost.

Benaud's own powers as a bowler were waning. His right shoulder seizing up like an old overused engine, no longer as flexible and supple as it once was. He started the '62-63 Ashes summer with a bang, but by the end had a series bowling average in excess of 40. The air was coming out of the tyre.

Apart from the next summer's Brisbane rain-drenched, Test against South Africa – a game blighted by Meckiff being called for throwing – the 1962-63 summer was Benaud's captaincy send-off.

He knew it had not finished as he had hoped. His disappointment, not at the overall series result, but the tempo and purpose of the cricket played had to be gleaned from his written comments and columns over the following years.

Benaud would never lay blame or overtly criticise his peers in his own side and opposition. That 5th Test on his home ground in Sydney, however, was not the final legacy he would have chosen in advance.

There's no need for any stimulus from above in 2025. The Ashes are a premium sporting product. People who want to go to English venues can't get in because of "sold out" signs. Even in Australia, apart from the MCG, houses in Sydney, Adelaide, Perth and Brisbane are full for the first three days of every Ashes Test. As they basically have been for the last 30 years.

There is no indication this will change in the foreseeable future.

Like a grotesque offspring shut away in the attic from outside view, the Ashes series of the '60s is only spoken about by the family in hushed tones. No one is supposed to know about it.

ACKNOWLEDGEMENTS

I wish to acknowledge the help of the following people who assisted me immeasurably in the writing of this book.

My thanks to the wonderful Greg Chappell for his outstanding foreword. Also, to Ken Piesse for his guidance and friendship.

I would also like to thank Michael Wilkinson and Jane Wilkinson at Wilkinson Publishing for their faith in this manuscript and Cassie Chiong, Chris McLeod and Paul Marcolin for ironing out the many glitches. And I especially want to acknowledge the charm and dignity of the great Test players from the 1960s who were so willing to chat to me about their time in the limelight and the issues arising from the Ashes cricket in that period.

To Tom Veivers, Doug Walters, Paul Sheahan, Mike Smith, Ken Eastwood and the late Barry Jarman, Geoff Pullar, Bob Simpson and Brian Booth my immense respect and gratitude. They were and are gentlemen of the highest class.

And finally to my closest and bestest cricket watching buddy, Craig Dunn. We have shared so much joy at the SCG, Adelaide Oval and MCG with, I am certain, many more delights to come.